INTO THE
MOUTHS OF
BABES

REVISED & UPDATED

A natural foods nutrition and feeding guide for infants and toddlers

Susan Tate Firkaly

BETTERWAY BOOKS

Cincinnati, Ohio

The information in this book has been prepared thoughtfully and care-fully. However, it is not intended to be prescriptive or diagnostic. Read-ers are asked to use their own good judgment and to consult their child's pediatrician or health-care provider when planning their children's diets.

Into the Mouths of Babes. Copyright © 1995 by Susan Tate Firkaly. Printed and bound in the United States of America. All rights reserved. No part of this book may be reproduced in any form or by any electronic or mechanical means including information storage and retrieval systems without permission in writing from the publisher, except by a reviewer, who may quote brief passages in a review. Published by Betterway Books, an imprint of F&W Publications, Inc., 1507 Dana Avenue, Cincinnati, Ohio, 45207. 1-800-289-0963. Second edition.

99 98 97 96 95   5 4 3 2 1

Library of Congress Cataloging-in-Publication Data

Firkaly, Susan Tate
    Into the mouths of babes : a natural foods nutrition and feeding guide for infants and toddlers / Susan Tate Firkaly. — 2nd ed.
        p.   cm.
    Includes bibliographical references and index.
    ISBN 1-55870-373-X (pbk.)
    1. Cookery (Baby foods)   2. Cookery (Natural foods)   3. Infants-Nutrition.
I. Title.
TX740.F53 1995
641.5'622 — dc20   94-45509
                                                                CIP

Edited by Hilary Swinson
Cover and interior design by Brian Roeth
Cover photo © 1994, Mike Malyszko, FPG International Corp.
Illustrations by Marion Reynolds, © 1984, 1994

About the Author

 Susan Tate Firkaly is an Assistant Professor in the School of Medicine at the University of Virginia where she is the Associate Director for Health Promotion in the Department of Student Health. She received her undergraduate degree in health education and physical education from Penn State University in 1971 and later earned a master's degree in health education administration from Kent State University. She is also the author of *AIDS and HIV Education: Effective Teaching Strategies* (V. Weston Walch, Publisher). Susan has lectured extensively across the country on a variety of health-related topics. As the mother of two teenagers, Zac and Molly, she has always enjoyed cooking wholesome foods for them and with them. Susan lives outside of Charlottesville, Virginia, with her sculptor husband and daughter.

I welcome comments, questions, baby photos and suggestions and will attempt to answer every correspondence. Please address your letter to:

Susan Tate Firkaly
Author — *Into the Mouths of Babes*
% F&W Publications
1507 Dana Avenue
Cincinnati, Ohio 45207

Acknowledgments

Without the support and encouragement of so many friends and family members who encouraged me in the initial writing of the first edition of this book, the second edition ten years later could not be a reality. Thank you all, once more, for each of your unique contributions.

A very special thank you:

to my parents, Helen and Ray Tate, for respecting my decision in feeding our children and for their never-ending supply of love,

to Ray Wunderlich, Jr., M.D., who again so willingly agreed to write the Foreword for this edition,

to Hilary Swinson, for her superior editorial expertise and insightfulness,

to William Brohaugh at F&W Publications, for believing in the merits of a second edition of this book,

to my Health Promotion colleagues at the University of Virginia's Department of Student Health, for their constant support and assistance, especially Marga Odahowski, Shari Levine and my administrative assistant, Reva Louise Crenshaw,

to Kelly Vollmer, M.D., for contributing her photographic skills,

to Molly and Zac, for the many gifts they share and for all I have learned from them, and

to my husband Michael, for always being there.

Dedicated to Zachary and Molly
my official taste-testers, mess-makers, and joy-givers!

CONTENTS

Foreword

Refreshing but especially reassuring is the news that Susan Tate Firkaly's children consistently choose to eat healthy foods. Now ten years after her first book, the fact that her children have not become junk-food addicts is evidence that her loving, nutritional counsel supplies the needs of children without obsessive deviations that lack "staying power."

For health reasons, recent guidelines for Americans advocate an increased consumption of whole grains, fruits and vegetables. One could not find a better way to implement that wisdom than to start *today* with good feeding of the babes, toddlers, preschoolers, schoolers and future parents of our land. Hence the supreme value of this carefully detailed and documented book.

Some, perhaps many readers of this book, may not elect to eat in an entirely vegetarian way. Nevertheless, the value of a high-quality diet as detailed herein can not be overemphasized. Whether one aims to be vegan, lacto-vegetarian, lacto-ovo-vegetarian or "near-vegetarian," the basic suggestions in Susan Firkaly's book are grist for the mill of good health. Her unique contribution is the combination of the best of academic learning with the experience of gentle caring for little people and the knowledge that "healthier eating" makes a difference.

In today's "rapid-fire," often hectic society, one must honestly ask this question: "How many parents are actually going to bother to put aside established convenience-eating to make their children's meals when already-prepared foods offer such an 'attractive' option?" The answer is that a growing wave (more than one-third of patients who see doctors) of health-conscious individuals has already turned to so-called "alternative" medicine to manage their departures from health. Many more seek healthy choices to prevent illness and thus avoid the need for expensive, after-the-fact, high-tech diagnosis and treatment. At a time when such "strange" modalities as antioxidants, herbs, homeopathic remedies, massage, exercise and prayer are increasingly used to blunt the accumulated ravages of stressful, fast-paced, convenience lifestyles, Susan Firkaly's modern counsel offers the practical dietary know-how that every family needs. Moreover, the marketplace today has responded so that healthy eating need not be the chore it once was.

Whether one adopts the entire approach or merely uses some of the ideas herein, this book is a prime resource for parents who need to tailor their childrens' diets away from the high load of sugared, salted, processed, chemically laden, high-animal-protein-containing foods to the wiser food choices spelled out here.

Healthy food for kids need not be sterile, flat and no fun. Susan Firkaly has seen to it that tasty *and* healthy foods can be primary staples, a vital ingredient for optimal nourishment. My experience over thirty-four years of medical and pediatric practice strongly indicates that eating in this way can only result in fewer allergies, behavior disorders, infectious diseases and later degenerative illness in those who—like Susan's children—continue the favorable eating habits that this book so cogently asserts.

Ray C. Wunderlich, Jr., B.S. M.D., B.A.

St. Petersburg, Florida

July, 1994

Preface to the Second Edition

It's been a decade since the printing of the first edition of *Into the Mouths of Babes* and somehow my little babes turned into teenagers, one of them living on his own. Little Zachary turned into Zac, the young man musician, and Molly now towers one inch above me at 5'8". As I reflect on the feeding choices I made, I am quite pleased with the result. Both Zac and Molly consistently *choose* to eat mostly healthy, unprocessed and vegetarian foods. Throughout this decade our family moved in and out of vegetarianism. When we were "out," we weren't "far out." But somehow we kept drifting back to plant protein instead of animal products — and we always felt better for it.

When my editor telephoned and asked if I could write an updated edition of this book, I was delighted to oblige. I have learned so much more about nutrition in the last ten years. Conflicting reports are still out there about what foods cause this and that, but the sound guidance offered in the original book has accurately stood the test of time.

I received many wonderful responses to the first edition through phone calls and letters from readers across the country. Actress Cybill Shepherd even telephoned me (Monday, May 16, 1988, to be exact) from a movie location in Washington, DC, to request an autographed copy of my book. Her cook was using a borrowed copy to prepare my recipes for her (then) new little twins, Ariel and Zack. I was thrilled, to say the least!

But the best result of writing this book has been watching our babies grow into healthy teenage people and feeling confident that they got off to the best nutritional start possible. The sound selection of natural foods they received throughout the years was validated for me when Zac requested a carrot cake for his eighteenth birthday. And I always smile when I watch Molly pack her own wholesome school lunches.

The original subtitle of the first edition was "A Natural Foods Cookbook for Infants and Toddlers." I often wondered about this choice of words for two reasons. One, obviously the infants weren't the ones reading the book and doing the cooking . . . and two, I always felt this was much more than a cookbook. Thus, we changed the description to more accurately reflect the book's contents, as this is truly a nutrition and feeding *guide* for those choosing natural foods for their baby.

One of the biggest changes in this edition is the news that choosing foods to obtain protein complementarity is easier than ever. The latest research indicates that we don't always need to combine proteins at the same meal. Protein needs can be met simply by eating a variety of plant proteins within several hours of each other. Plant sources are recognized more than ever for their disease-preventing power and their excellent sources of protein and calcium.

Since my first edition was written, the USDA has changed the "Basic Four" food groups into a "Food Pyramid," reflecting the importance of eating more whole grains, fruits and vegetables and reducing the number of servings of meat and dairy products. This had no effect on the vegetarians who were aware of this fact long ago and were already choosing to eat a healthy variety of grains, fruits and vegetables. The "Meatless Four Food Groups" illustrated and described in the original edition are still an accurate guide for those lacto-ovo vegetarians who include dairy products in their diet. I changed the name of this chart to the "Vegetarian Four" to emphasize what was included *in* these groups rather than left *out* of them.

A most notable addition to this book is the inclusion of the "New Four Food Groups" guidelines developed and recommended by the Physicians Committee for Responsible Medicine (PCRM) in 1991. This is an excellent guide for vegans (vegetarians who obtain their protein and calcium from plant sources only and do not eat any animal products).

As it was in the first edition, the "Allergy Basic Four" chart is included to help plan menus for children with allergies. This fourth chart rounds out the selection of food guides you will find in chapter five.

For the past five years I have worked in the college health field as a health education administrator. The noticeable recognition of eating disorders on college campuses has resulted in an expanded section on disordered eating and body dissatisfaction in chapter six. The American "thin is in" culture has only become worse since pictures of a young, skinny Twiggy appeared in the 1960s. Too many girls of the 1990s have felt compelled to starve themselves (resulting in anorexia), to binge and purge (resulting in bulimia) or to compulsively eat (known as binge-eating) to try to obtain the unreal image of what they now see daily on photographically altered magazine photos, videos and TV images created with costly special effects. Since these adolescent girls (and some boys) who have had disordered eating habits may eventually become mothers (and fathers), I felt it necessary to discuss what consequences this might have on the nutritional choices and attitudes accompanying the wonders of new parenthood.

Since the original edition was published in 1984, the best compliment I have received about my book was from a young mother who told me *Into the Mouths of Babes* was a lifesaver for her because it provided a comprehensive feeding guide that was supportive and guilt-free while it helped her through those often scary moments when she was trying to figure out if she was doing everything right. This constant support and encouragement remains the common thread of this book. I wish you many happy feeding, growing and loving times together.

Susan Tate Firkaly

July, 1994

Introduction

Somewhere around the middle of my first pregnancy, it occurred to me that I soon would have the task of deciding what to feed our baby. When to give vegetables? How soon to give whole milk? How much milk should be given? How often? While studying everything I could on pregnancy and childbirth (through the eyes of a mother and a professional health educator), I also began the search for answers to my questions, which resulted in my extensive study of infant nutrition.

I spent years scrutinizing pages of information and ideas on infant feeding and found amazing contradictions in numerous areas. Where conflicting informed opinions existed between starting ages for a certain food, I chose the later starting date. Children have their entire lives to eat a variety of foods. I saw no reason to rush the introduction of too many foods too early and thereby risk possible allergic reactions.

The purpose of this book is to provide supportive direction, information on infant nutrition and feeding, and a variety of whole food recipes that can be used instead of or along with prepared baby food. Although there is no single right way to feed your baby, *Into the Mouths of Babes* can be used as a guide to feeding your infant, along with your own instincts and advice from your health-care provider.

Mothers, fathers and other caregivers can easily follow these recipes. Most books assume the mother prepares food for "her" baby. Today, many more fathers take an active role in all aspects of parenting. Sex-biased and stereotyped books on child-rearing and feeding are unfair to the many fathers at home with their children, or to partners sharing child-rearing responsibilities with the mother. With this in mind, I often use the word "parent," "grown-up" or "caregiver" instead of "mother."

Many parents prefer opening a jar and feeding their babies with only seconds of preparation. Can they be blamed, with only twenty-four hours in a day and a baby taking up twenty-three? Many of the nutritious recipes presented here are as quick and easy to prepare as store-bought products. There are also recipes for preparing large batches of food that can be frozen for later use. Whether working inside or outside the home, we all need time-saving ideas so we're not chained to the high chair.

Since the birth of our first child, Zachary, over eighteen years ago, our family gradually developed a change in eating habits, from the typical meat and potatoes menu to more natural foods and a meatless diet. The expense of meat alone has caused many of us to look for cost-saving but nutritious alternatives. Increasing awareness of global hunger and the environment, and our respect for animals and their rights have pointed out the positive results of a vegetarian diet. When I learned that meat was even more difficult for an infant to digest than for an adult, it was easy to make the decision not to feed our babies meat.

We began to change our diet by including a meatless meal every other night in menu planning. As we gradually moved to a vegetarian diet, we found we felt better after eating. Our digestive systems didn't need to work as hard to digest and eliminate plant protein, and we actually felt more energetic after meals instead of overfed and ready for a nap. We also liked not eating chemically fattened animals.

Many parents will choose to wait until after the first year to introduce meat while others will choose to raise their child on a vegetarian or vegan diet. The information in this book can be a guide for you regardless of your choice, although these recipes contain no meat. It is important to be comfortable with your choice and knowledgeable about whatever eating plan you may choose.

Realizing the need to provide ample protein in our meatless diets caused us to learn more about other foods or food combinations high in protein. Frances Moore Lappe's 1975 version of *Diet for a Small Planet* was of immense help to me when our children were young. Her twentieth anniversary edition published in 1991 provides the latest updated information about protein complementarity—the proper combination of plant proteins or nonmeat animal protein to achieve a quality protein equal to or better than meat sources. (See chapter five.)

I developed these recipes for our family by using such food combinations as rice and beans, wheat and milk, and beans and cheese. The initial challenge soon became routine. Feeling good about Zachary's diet, I began to collect the recipes I used for his meals. When Molly was born in 1980, I devised even more recipes and concoctions for her. As my recipes and knowledge of infant nutrition expanded, and scraps of paper overflowed my recipe box, I realized others might benefit from what I had learned. After laboring for several years, I finally was able to give birth to the first edition of *Into the Mouths of Babes* in 1984. Ten years later I am happy to present this expanded and updated edition to you, feeling quite pleased with the nutritional health of our children, who are now teenagers.

The recipes are divided into six chapters: "Beginner Recipes" (starting at age six months); "Intermediate Recipes" (for ages seven to nine months); "Advanced Recipes" (ages ten to twelve months); "Toddle Food" (ages one to two); "Whole-Family Recipes" which provides wholesome recipes for all ages so that a natural progression from infancy can be continued; and "Recipes for the Allergic Child" which includes suggestions for preparing food when allergies must be considered.

Preparation time varies but many of the recipes can be prepared in ten minutes or less. The recipes that take a little longer to prepare can be planned easily around your family's meal for that day. Although I love to cook I always found menu-planning an unlikable chore. I also found it is worth taking ten to fifteen minutes to plan a weekly menu rather than sighing and groaning around the kitchen just prior to meal-time. (Okay, I must admit, after all these years, I still wait until the last minute all too frequently.) Having family members call out their suggestions to you can be quite a help and also lets everyone share in the "fun" of menu-planning. Sharing this task (as well as the cooking) helps other family members take part in this responsibility.

Before the recipe chapters you will find information on how, what and when to feed your baby. This book also includes basic information needed to understand the basics of nutrition, with special emphasis on infant nutrition. A chapter about prenatal nutrition, "Into the Mouths of Future Moms," precedes the chapter on infant nutrition.

Along with information for infant and prenatal nutrition there also are four important food charts to help in your menu-planning: the new Food Pyramid (replacing the USDA's old four food groups), the Vegetarian Food Groups for meatless diets, the New Four Food Groups for vegans, and the Allergy Basic Four.

The chapter entitled "Coping with Food Allergies" can help those who need guidelines for planning meals when food choices are limited. It includes information and guidance that can help parents and children in dealing with food substances that often cause harmful reactions.

I have written this book so I could share nutritional information and recipes with others concerned about foods their children eat. With the exception of the recipes in the allergy section, each recipe has been taste-tested by our children and has met with their approval.

Good nutrition can be a lifelong gift to our children. As parents we have the responsibility to provide nourishment that will help our beautiful little people blossom into unique, healthy big people. It is my hope that the recipes and ideas in this book will help in providing your child with the best start possible for a healthful journey through life.

Chapter One

WHY MAKE YOUR OWN BABY FOOD?

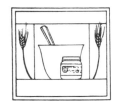

I n this high-tech age of microwave ovens and ready-prepared foods, why bother making your own baby food? It is so easy to open a jar, but the comparison between what is in that jar and what is in home-prepared "Baby's Own" is quite noteworthy.

NUTRITIONAL QUALITY

The nutritional superiority of a homemade product probably is the best reason to make your own. The concerned parent who elects to make baby food from scratch can choose fresh vegetables, fruits and grains to serve without adding any unnecessary ingredients. Homemade products don't need preservatives to lengthen shelf life, because they are eaten fresh daily or quickly frozen for later use.

ECONOMY

It's more economical! When making one's own baby food, there is no expense for the jars, labor, bright packaging, advertising or "extra" ingredients. The cost of a baby food jar alone often comprises one-third of the cost passed on to the consumer. Many commercial jars of food contain water and the consumer pays for that liquid weight. Of course homemade foods contain water, but it's your water, prepared along with your fresh ingredients. We can often purchase foods for our baby from the grocer's "adult food" shelves, not only from the baby food aisle. Buying regular natural juices instead of baby juice will save on the grocery bill. Those juices can be diluted a bit at home (or strained in the case of orange juice) and given to your baby.

CONTROL OF INGREDIENTS

Many commercially prepared baby foods contain "modified starch" to keep the food from separating and to act as a thickening agent. This starch is treated with acids in the process of being made into this unnecessary additive.

Some of the baby foods on your grocer's shelves still contain salt and sugar. The increased nutritional awareness of consumers, however, has forced companies to remove these unnecessary ingredients from most of their baby foods.

There is one ingredient that neither Gerber nor Heinz adds — and that ingredient is your *love*. Preparing and sharing food, especially with your own family, feels good, and being able to add that loving touch feels even better. The satisfaction of knowing the food you make contains only the best ingredients is yet another reason to make your own.

Some of these recipes take longer to prepare than others. It would be wise to prepare them when spare time allows so that, on a daily basis, less preparation would be needed. As an example, oats can be ground in a food processor or blender, placed in a clean jar, labeled, and then used as needed. Batches of vegetables can be made up all at one time, frozen in ice cube trays (see chapter two, "Your Kitchen Layette") and used later. Most other recipes take ten to fifteen minutes or less. The time, energy and caring it takes to prepare these foods can be considered a daily gift of good nutrition to your child.

DETERMINE WHAT'S RIGHT FOR YOU AND YOUR BABY

Giving your child nutritious foods that are served in a loving, peaceful manner is much more important than knocking yourself out trying to make every single food that enters your baby's mouth. It's so important to feel comfortable in your role as "dietitian" for your child. Some people might be happy making fruits and vegetables but buying prepared cereals rather than grinding and cooking their own grains. That's great! Some people might buy some foods and make homemade foods when they have time. That's great too! Others may choose to make everything from scratch. There is no single absolutely right way of feeding your baby. Make choices that suit you and your life-style. Whichever way you opt for — have fun!

Chapter Two

YOUR KITCHEN LAYETTE

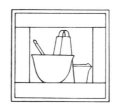

Clean hands, utensils and cookware in the kitchen are vital to the preparation of safe homemade baby food. Take inventory of the cookware, storage and serving equipment you already have, and then add any of the following items from the following lists that will help to complete your "kitchen layette."

It is not necessary to have all of these items in order to make your baby's food, just as it is not imperative that a baby have six side-snap undershirts, four kimonos, six sleepers, four receiving blankets and six pairs of plastic pants.

After you read through some recipes, use your own judgment to decide what you will need.

To Prepare:

Baby food grinder
Blender
Grater
Steam basket

Food mill
Food processor
Pressure cooker

To Store:

Ice cube trays
Plastic freezer or bottle bags
Glass jars

To Serve:

Bib
Baby spoon
High chair
Spouted cup
Heated baby dish

To Travel:

Lunch box
Thermos

Baby food grinder. A vital necessity! Ask anyone who has ever used one — they're great! For use at home, just put the foods you want pureed into the cylinder, grind and serve right from the grinder. Whip it out at a restaurant or at a friend's house for dinner, and add the foods you select for your baby. It's like carrying a miniature blender in your purse or diaper bag. These are inexpensive (under ten dollars) and are worth every penny.

Blender. A great timesaving appliance if you seriously plan to prepare your baby's food. It doesn't have to have eighteen speeds — any old blender that "blends" will do.

Grater. A small hand grater is needed for some of the vegetable recipes. A food processor would be a real treat to have, but a grater works "great."

Steam basket. A collapsible steam basket is needed for cooking vegetables with steam. This inexpensive basket fits inside a saucepan containing about an inch of water. (Water should not touch the vegetables.) After covering the saucepan with a tight-fitting lid, steaming vegetables over medium heat is an easy way to cook. There is no need to stir. Steaming (but not overcooking) is a good way to save the valuable vitamin content in vegetables.

Food mill. These are larger versions of the baby food grinder, allowing larger quantities of foods to be blended at one time. While not a necessity, a food mill can be useful in preparing baby food, particularly if a blender or food processor is not already in your kitchen.

Food processor. If you are interested in saving time in the kitchen, this appliance is a delight. It blends, purees, grates or grinds a larger amount than the blender. A food processor is not necessary for baby food making, but it saves time in many ways.

Pressure cooker. This timesaving, nutrient-saving device is wonderful for cooking large batches of fruits, vegetables and other foods. Although a pressure cooker is not essential to preparing these foods, it is a big help. Many people fear these because they've heard horror stories about the lids flying off sending green beans all over the ceiling. A pressure cooker need not be feared if: (1) you read and follow the directions, and (2) you don't leave the pressure cooker on while you go out grocery shopping.

People who use their pressure cookers love them. A new style of pressure cooker was introduced in the mid-1980s using a stationary pressure regulator rather than the original jiggle-top kind. Their safety has improved dramatically over the older version and they are easier to use. If you own one made before these improvements, check to be sure the rubber gasket is in good condition and not brittle. (New gaskets are available at housewares sections in larger department stores.) Check Lorna Sass's book, *Recipes from an Ecological Kitchen*, listed in the bibliography section of this book for more ideas and instructions about pressure cookers. Dust off that pressure cooker you received as a wedding gift, read the directions, and pride yourself on finding another way to save time in the kitchen.

Ice cube trays. A few ice cube trays are needed for freezing large quantities of fruits and vegetables. As soon as the cubes are frozen, plop them into a plastic bag, label, date and keep in the freezer.

Plastic freezer bags. These can be used to hold the various frozen food cubes prepared in your kitchen. They are clean and designed for freezer use. Be sure to label each bag. It's amazing how things can get lost in a freezer. The individual, sterile plastic baby bottle bags are wonderful to hold frozen food cubes to take traveling, whether out to a friend's for lunch or on a five-hour trip to see the grandparents.

MICROWAVE SAFETY TIPS

If you are using a microwave to heat baby's food, be sure to stir after heating and then test the food yourself before serving. Microwaves heat unevenly and one bite of food may be hotter (or cooler) than another bite. Do *not* heat baby bottles in the microwave. The uneven heating can result in serious burns for your little one.

Glass jars. Sterile glass jars (canning jars or peanut butter jars) are good for storing ground oats and other grains. Remember to label each jar, or you will be astonished at how everything looks the same next time you check your shelf.

Bib. Unless you're a masochist, a few bibs on hand go a long way in saving your sanity. They eliminate (almost) food stains (watch out for peaches and bananas) and keep your baby from getting sticky and gooey (at least where the bib is).

Baby spoon. A slender spoon made just for baby's mouth must be much easier than an adult-sized spoon. (Imagine eating your cereal from a large serving spoon — good tasting, but mouth stretching!) Some babies seem to prefer plastic-coated spoons; others are just glad they are fed.

High chair. A high chair is a wonderful invention. It provides baby with a comfortable place to eat and grownups with a little bit of breathing time. Be sure baby is secured safely in the seat belt but never assume your baby won't slip out or stand up and fall out of the chair. The tray provides a nice place for finger foods that baby can reach for or push all over the floor. An old plastic tablecloth placed beneath the high chair is an excellent floor or carpet saver.

Spouted cup. A small cup with lid and spout top is great for introducing the cup to your six-month-old baby. By eight to nine months, the idea of a cup can be second nature. Encourage your baby to hold the cup. Many children are weaned from breast milk or the bottle at twelve months and go successfully to the cup. Avoid buying the weighted "no-tip" cups. They're often too heavy or awkward for a baby to pick up easily.

Heated baby dish. This is helpful and convenient, but not a necessity. A heated dish is great for melting your frozen food cubes, but a small saucepan (egg poaching size) or microwave oven will do the job fine. Any small bowl can be used to serve the food.

Lunch box. A lunch box to carry little food cubes, pieces of cheese, fruit or a thermos of juice when going out is really useful. Infants and children who spend some of their day with a day care provider or attending preschool can have access to the healthy foods you pack. Packing a lunch to take to a restaurant or friend's house assures your child is eating the foods you choose for him. Plastic, metal or thermal-lined lunch boxes all work well. Remember to include a bib, spoon, baby cup and wet washcloth for quick face and hand cleaning when going out to a restaurant or out for the afternoon. (A wet washcloth in a plastic bag added to a purse, backpack, diaper bag or lunch box saves money on baby wipes and comes in handy.)

Thermos. Inside every lunch box can be a thermos for baby's soup, cereal, or juice. Many restaurants do not have a good juice selection so having a thermos handy will guarantee your child of a nutritious drink wherever you go.

Chapter Three

A SHOPPER'S GUIDE TO WHOLE FOODS

Anatural foods diet for baby should contain a variety of healthy foods. This chapter contains a guide to whole foods that can be substituted for processed, bleached, refined or artificial foods.

Before my children were born many of the "natural" foods listed below were not in our kitchen cupboards. Today these items are often on our grocery list.

Yogurt	Whole wheat flour
Tofu	Barley
Dry milk	Soybeans
Garbanzo beans	Lentils
Spinach	Sprouts
Honey	Bulgur
Sesame seeds	Rice cakes
Granola	Pita bread
Avocado	

THE NEW LABELING

When choosing packaged foods for ourselves or baby, it is good to know what nutrients they contain. In the early 1990s, the Food and Drug Administration (FDA) developed a more accurate and consistent food labeling system that requires food packages to contain a "Nutrition Facts" food label. This label contains information about serving size along with the amount and percentage of the daily value of fat, cholesterol, sodium, carbohydrate and protein each serving contains. It must also list the percentage of vitamins A and C plus two minerals, calcium and iron, along with the percent of the daily value this serving provides. (Many companies choose to list other vitamins and minerals too.) Some labels have even added the number of calories per gram of fat, carbohydrate and protein. The label also includes a list of all ingredients, in descending order of concentration.

It remains optional for companies to provide nutritional information for fresh fruit, vegetables and bulk foods. If you need more information about specific nutrients in these foods you can refer to *The Wellness Encyclopedia of Food and Nutrition* or *The Healing Foods* (both listed in the bibliography).

ADDING WHOLESOME FOODS

The chart on the next page offers some suggestions for substitutions that will provide your family with a more nutritious, wholesome diet. If you have eaten very few of these foods and at first glance find many of the baby food recipes unusual, you are not alone. If you want to feed your child natural foods and are attempting to change your own diet, try adding these foods to your menu slowly. Trying one or two new foods a week will help you more than sitting down to a dinner of bulgur, zucchini, sesame seeds, tofu and sprouts!

NATURAL COLORS AND FLAVORINGS

Read the label to find out if these are natural or synthetic. Unfortunately, many prepared foods found at the supermarket contain synthetic additives. Artificial colors and flavorings are now known to be contributing causes of hyperactivity and learning disabilities in children. Many adults and children have allergic reactions when they eat foods containing chemical additives. Natural additives include: colorings from vegetable juices, herbs, spices, salt, fresh fruit acids, brewer's yeast and wheat germ.

FRESH VEGETABLES

Fresh vegetables surpass canned vegetables in flavor and nutrition. Using the pressure cooker will save time and nutrients. Shop for fresh, organic and undamaged vegetables.

Better Nutrition Substitutions

Instead of	Substitute
artificial colors, flavors	natural colors and flavors
canned vegetables	fresh vegetables
chocolate	carob
colored cheeses	white, natural cheeses
cornstarch	arrowroot
double-acting baking powder	single-acting baking powder
hydrogenated peanut butter	fresh, natural peanut butter
mayonnaise	safflower mayonnaise, homemade mayonnaise
meat	nonmeat protein combinations
prepared packaged cereals	natural cereals, your own cooked grain cereals
refined oil	safflower, peanut, corn, soybean or sunflower oil
vanilla flavoring	vanilla extract
salt	sea salt
sugar	honey, molasses
white cornmeal	yellow cornmeal
white flour	whole wheat flour
white rice	brown rice

CAROB

Carob is made from ground pods of the honey locust tree. Although it looks like chocolate, it does not contain caffeine, sugar, vanillin or emulsifiers. Babies who never have tasted chocolate (and they should not have any before the age of three) find a carob drink quite a treat. For us chocolate lovers, it takes experimenting with carob for a while to discover it can be quite likable.

Carob powder (sometimes called carob flour) is low in fat and offers valuable minerals, unlike its chocolate "cousin." Carob is a bit sweeter than cocoa, so you need to reduce the amount of sweetener if substituting carob powder in some of your favorite chocolate recipes.

NATURAL CHEESE

Processed cheeses usually can be spotted quickly by their orange or yellow color. Good old American cheese is made from natural cheeses, but before it is packaged it is ground, blended, emulsified, heated, artificially colored, mixed with water or milk solids — and sometimes preservatives — then pressed into a smooth plastic-like mass. Natural cheeses contain "real" ingredients: milk, rennin (a natural enzyme) and lactic acid bacteria (to sour the milk naturally). Swiss, provolone, Monterey Jack, cheddar and brick are examples of good, natural cheeses.

ARROWROOT

Arrowroot is a tasteless white powder that can be used as a thickening for gravies and sauces. It may be substituted in equal amounts for cornstarch or white flour (both are bleached products). It is easily digestible and also adds minerals.

BAKING POWDER

Double-acting powder contains aluminum compounds, whereas single-acting baking powder contains an acidic ingredient (tartaric acid) and baking soda. Researchers have been concerned for many years about the possible toxicity in consuming aluminum in our foods. To be on the safe side, use the single-acting kind.

PEANUT BUTTER

Natural peanut butter contains peanuts and sometimes salt. Most brands found on your grocer's shelf are hydrogenated (artificially hardened) to help keep the peanut oil from separating. Sweeteners also are added to commercially prepared peanut butter. A quick stir of the jar of natural peanut butter makes everything look fine and your family comes out ahead.

SAFFLOWER MAYONNAISE

Most supermarket mayonnaise contains preservatives and additives. If you don't want to make your own, purchase safflower mayonnaise to use in your favorite recipes.

PROTEIN

Using grains, legumes and milk products in proper combination is a healthy replacement for meat. Livestock raised for human consumption too frequently contains unacceptable levels of toxic pesticides and herbicides, antibiotics or synthetic hormones. (See chapter five, "Infant Nutrition," for additional information about nonmeat alternatives.)

NATURAL CEREALS

Can breakfast exist without sugar-coated, artificially colored cereals? Fortunately, the answer is "yes." There are two general choices.

The first is to buy prepared cereals in a health food store or in the natural food section of your grocery store. Although several varieties exist, it still is necessary to read the cereal labels. Do not assume it is natural, sugarfree, additive-free or preservative-free just because you found it in the natural food section. Check the list at the end of this chapter for suggestions.

Making cereal from grains is easy and another way to provide baby and family with a wholesome breakfast. Oats, rice and cornmeal can be cooked into delicious cereals. One packaged natural cereal that was popular with our children when they were younger is a wheat cereal called Bear Mush. Cleverly named and packaged (little bears on the package eating porridge) by Arrowhead Mills, this cereal is a real hit with children. Bear Mush sounds a lot more exciting to toddlers than Cream of Wheat!

UNREFINED OILS

Unrefined oils include safflower, sunflower, sesame, soybean, corn, canola, olive, peanut and wheat germ oil. In refining oil, vitamin E is removed and preservatives added. Safflower oil is a mild, inexpensive, almost tasteless oil that can easily be substituted for any refined oil.

VANILLA EXTRACT

Imitation vanilla flavoring and vanillin are both artificial substitutes for pure vanilla. Using vanilla extract in recipes makes a distinct difference you will enjoy.

SEA SALT

Babies do not need salt. Children and adults do not need a lot of salt, especially if hypertension is a problem. Regular table salt contains anti-caking chemicals to keep the salt flowing freely and sodium bicarbonate to keep it white. Sea salt is just that: sea salt. It offers the minerals that are taken out in the refining of table salt. Using herbs and spices to flavor foods and realizing that many foods naturally contain sodium can be one more step toward overall good health.

HONEY AND MOLASSES

Honey or molasses can be used to replace sugar in most recipes. Uncooked honey has caused botulism and even death in children under age one. Do *not* feed infants uncooked honey before age one!

Nutritional awareness has caused many parents to cut back the amount of sugar they give their children. Recent research has resulted in some doubt about the widespread belief that sugar can cause hyperactivity in children. When these studies are done without the funding by food companies and when parents tell me sugar actually calms their children, I'll consider believing their results.

What is so bad about sugar? Sugar contributes nothing of nutritional value to the body; in fact, it takes away valuable B-vitamins during the digestive process. Sugar also rots teeth, adds weight and can cause jangled nerves.

We all seem to crave something sweet now and then. How can a sweet tooth be satisfied? Fresh fruit contains natural sweeteners and is healthier than a candy bar.

How can foods be sweetened without sugar? Honey is a great substitute (for ages one and older) because it is a natural product from the nectar of flowers. Because honey is sweeter than sugar, you don't need to use as much. Honey causes foods to brown faster so baking time might need to be shortened. Decrease the amount of other liquids by one-fourth cup for each cup of honey used.

Molasses is another good sweetener. It is high in B vitamins and a good source of calcium and iron.

YELLOW CORNMEAL

White cornmeal is degerminated, bleached, stripped of its original vitamins and then synthetically enriched. Natural yellow cornmeal (often labeled "unbolted") contains more vitamin A than commercial, degerminated cornmeal.

WHOLE WHEAT FLOUR

Whole wheat flour contains vitamins B and E, protein, iron and phosphorus. It does not need to be "enriched" since nature already did its job. The wheat bran and wheat germ are milled out of white flour, causing a loss of fiber. White flour also is bleached and enriched to synthetically replace some of the nutrients taken out during processing.

It is best to purchase whole wheat flour in small quantities and store it in the refrigerator to ensure freshness. If exposed to warm temperatures it can spoil more quickly, resulting in a bad taste and odor.

For each cup of white flour needed, replace with ¾ cup whole wheat flour. If white flour has been a part of your household for years, make the change gradually. First switch to unbleached flour (this is one step up from white flour since it was spared the bleaching process). Then try substituting one-half cup unbleached flour and one-half cup whole wheat flour for each cup of white flour you once used. For most people this gradual change is easily accepted.

BROWN RICE

White rice is another example of a whole grain being robbed of its important nutrients. Brown rice is a nutritionally superior grain well worth the extra time it takes to prepare. Cooking time for brown rice is about forty-five minutes, but it is good time invested in providing baby, yourself and the rest of your family with another natural, whole food. Brown rice freezes well so make extra and freeze in one-cup portions for later use. Basmati rice is a naturally white whole-grain rice that cooks in twenty minutes and has a nice nutty flavor. It is a good substitute when moving from white rice to brown rice.

A TRIP TO THE HEALTH FOOD STORE

If you plan to purchase many of the above foods for the first time, the most economical way is at a health food store or through a food cooperative. Many large supermarkets now include a natural food section so that a special trip is not needed. Some newer supermarket chains, such as Fresh Fields, stock *only* natural foods that must meet rigorous criteria for selection. Their "bulk" food section has prepackaged foods already measured and labeled in simple, less expensive packaging.

Have you avoided shopping in "health food" or "natural food" stores because they look different from your regular supermarket? Here are a few tips to guide you through your first visit.

The biggest difference between a health food store and a regular supermarket is what is on the shelves. The wonderful bins of whole grains, beans, rice, dried fruits and nuts are there for you to measure just as much as you want. Because you, the consumer, do the measuring, bagging and often price labeling, you are the one to pocket the savings. (Note: Not all "health food" products are cheaper. Shop around and make sure you are not paying for pretty packaging or health food fads.)

Be sure the health food store you choose maintains superior sanitary conditions. If you have any doubts as to the freshness or source of any foods, ask the manager or return questionable items.

To many people, health food stores can be a bit intimidating. One way to become familiar with the store is to have a friend or neighbor take you along on a shopping trip. If this isn't possible, stop in one day just to browse. Watch what people are doing, how they bag the food, whether they are writing a price on the package, where things are and what items cost. If you see something you want, measure what you need and march up to the cashier with your purchase. The next time you shop there, it will be more familiar. Most sales associates are more than willing to help you—so go ahead and ask.

Good Foods for Baby or Toddler
A Supermarket* Shopper's Guide

Fruits and Juices	Some Good Brands
Applesauce	Any sugarfree, 100% natural supermarket brand, Eden
Fruit juices	After the Fall, Lakewood, Escondido, Ferraro's, Knudsen, Cascadian Farm, Just Pik't Juice, Earth's Best
Frozen grape juice	Seneca (sugarfree)
Jams/Spreads	**Some Good Brands**
Apple butter	Tap'n Apple, Eden, Shiloh Farms, Orchard's Best
Peanut butter	Arrowhead Mills
Nut butters (sesame [tahini], almond, peanut, cashew)	Westbrae, Joyva, Roaster Fresh, Arrowhead Mills, Once Again Nut Butters
Jams, fruit spreads	Crofters, Cascadian Farm, Sorrell Ridge
Breads/Crackers	**Some Good Brands**
Rice cakes	Westbrae Natural, Lundberg, Hain
Whole wheat pita bread	Any 100% whole wheat
Biscuits for toddlers	Healthy Times
100% whole wheat honey graham crackers	Mi-Del
100% wheat crackers	Health Valley
Rye Norwegian flatbread	Kavli
Crackers	Ryvita, Health Valley, Auburn Farms, Hain
Crisp bread	Wasa

Dairy Products	Some Good Brands
Yogurt	Alta Dena, Stonyfield, Brown Cow
Organic yogurt	Horizons
Dairyless yogurt	White Wave
Cereals	**Some Good Brands**
Old-fashioned oats	Quaker, Arrowhead Mills
Puffed cereals (rice, wheat, millet and corn)	Arrowhead Mills
Oat bran	Nature's Path, Erewhon, Health Valley
Nature O's	Arrowhead Mills
Familia Baby Cereal	Familia
Muesli	Familia, Golden Temple
Brown Rice or Corn Lites	Health Valley
Bear Mush	Arrowhead Mills
7 Grain Cereal	Arrowhead Mills
Natural cereal for babies	Health Valley, Earth's Best
Prepared Baby Food	Earth's Best

* Most large supermarkets have a natural food section. Be sure to ask the manager to order foods you need but do not see on the grocer's shelves.

Notes on Favorite Natural Foods

Product/Brand	Purchased From
_____	_____
_____	_____
_____	_____
_____	_____
_____	_____
_____	_____
_____	_____
_____	_____
_____	_____
_____	_____
_____	_____
_____	_____
_____	_____
_____	_____
_____	_____
_____	_____
_____	_____
_____	_____

Chapter Four

INTO THE MOUTHS OF FUTURE MOMS

I n the beginning, or even before the conception of your baby, nutrition plays a vital role in the creation of a healthy newborn. "Future moms" are increasingly aware that careful selection of wholesome foods is a real plus when the goal is a healthy baby. Months (even years) before conception, women are becoming selective about the food and drink they consume. Many prospective mothers take a good look at their bodies and wisely reduce or eliminate sugar, caffeine, alcohol and smoking. They exercise to strengthen their bodies, the soon-to-be home of their offspring. The coffee and doughnut breakfast, missed lunch and highly processed dinner are replaced by meals that provide quality in every bite. The future mom does this because of the realization that she is the one responsible for the nourishment that passes through her womb to the baby. Whewwww ... heavy responsibility comes so soon when two join together to create another little mouth to feed!

WEIGHT GAIN

One of the early concerns of a pregnant woman is weight gain. Most health-care providers recommend an average gain of between twenty-five and thirty-five pounds. The pattern of weight gain, as well as the amount, is also important. Many women dread this "heavier" part of pregnancy, thinking they just don't want to look fat. Don't worry though; there is a *big* difference between being fat and being pregnant.

Being pregnant causes a woman to add a nice big bulge around the front of her body—there's another living creature inside! Breasts become larger as they begin to prepare for the very first (and homemade!)

baby food. Without adding this roundness to the upper and lower parts of her body, it would be somewhat difficult to give birth. This leads to a very special little human being with whom you get to share your life. Most women think the extra weight is a great trade for the end result!

When the baby pops out (oh, if it were only that simple) a woman immediately loses about ten pounds: baby's weight, placenta, plus some fluids. After the health-care provider gives the okay at the postpartum exam, a woman can gradually resume exercise and physical activities that will help to shed the remaining excess weight. If the woman chooses to nurse, her breasts will remain larger and her uterus will return to normal shape rather quickly.

NUTRITION FOR A PREGNANT WOMAN

What should a pregnant woman eat? Basically, the same wholesome foods required by healthy adults, but more of them. When pregnant, a woman is eating for two so what she does or doesn't eat affects both mother and child. Baby's nutritional needs are taken care of first with any "extra" nutrients passed to the mother—so be careful not to short-change either.

The need for protein increases dramatically (about 30 percent) during pregnancy. The developing brain cells of the baby depend on constant protein intake. During the last three months of pregnancy, there occurs an even greater need for protein because of the baby's rapidly growing body. If a pregnant woman falls short of her required protein intake, toxemia could occur. Toxemia is a disorder during pregnancy that results in a rise in blood pressure, swelling of ankles and other body parts, and protein in the urine. This serious condition can be dangerous to both infant and mother, so constant prenatal care is a must. This is why blood pressure, a warning signal of toxemia, is monitored closely during prenatal exams.

Calcium Needs

During pregnancy, a woman needs to be sure to consume at least 1200 milligrams of calcium each day. Eating at least four servings of calcium-rich foods each day is a must. Four glasses of skim milk in the daily diet is one way for pregnant women to obtain adequate amounts of calcium if you eat dairy products. Drinking skim milk also allows room for more calories in another part of the diet. If milk is not a favorite drink or you are lactose intolerant, try substituting acidophilus milk, certain herbal teas and eating more calcium-rich foods such as leafy greens. If you do not include dairy products in your diet be sure to choose from almond butter, beans, calcium-fortified soymilk (check the label to see what percentage of the daily allowance is supplied in one glass), cereals, and juices, dark green leafy vegetables, figs, sunflower seeds, tahini or tofu.

If you obtain your protein source solely from plant foods, be sure vitamin B_{12} is in your daily multivitamin or that you eat one serving each day of a food that contains or is fortified with this essential nutrient. Miso and tempeh fermented with Klebsiella bacteria contain B_{12}. If you don't eat foods fortified with vitamin D, it is suggested that you get twenty to thirty minutes of direct sunlight (the natural source of vitamin D) on your hands, arms and face at least three times a week.

Iron Needs

Along with paying particular attention to protein, calcium, vitamin B_{12} and vitamin D needs, a pregnant woman must be careful to eat enough foods that contain iron, especially in the second half of pregnancy. The growing fetus will be storing the iron needed for the first six months after birth. This is one of the reasons health-care providers prescribe the large vitamin-mineral pill pregnant women "love" to take daily. The iron contained in this supplement is a little added insurance to help meet nutritional requirements.

The following foods are high in iron and can help prevent anemia (iron deficiency) during pregnancy: whole grains, beans, dried fruits, dark green vegetables, sunflower seeds, seafood and blackstrap molasses. An afternoon snack of dried fruits and some nuts is a healthy and satisfying treat.

Folic Acid

Folic acid (folacin) deficiency is another condition that often occurs. Along with protein, folic acid, a member of the vitamin B complex group, is being used to help form large amounts of baby's new tissues. So much is needed during pregnancy that the Recommended Daily Allowance is 800 micrograms during pregnancy, twice what is normally required. The best natural sources of folic acid include carrots, egg yolk, dark green leafy vegetables, avocados, apricots and whole wheat flour.

MANAGING STRESS

Recently many researchers have discovered the ill effects stress can cause the unborn baby. Stress seems to deplete B vitamins so quickly that it often causes a pregnant woman to become deficient in this very important group of vitamins. It is difficult to have a stress-free pregnancy, but every effort should be made to deal with stress by keeping a positive mental attitude and a good diet filled with B vitamins. Pamper yourself by making time to do things that help you feel more relaxed. Moderate exercise (unless restricted by your care provider) releases endorphins that can make you feel great. Avoid exercising on an empty stomach (a rapid drop in blood sugar can occur) and drink plenty of water during your exercise and afterward to replace all fluid lost during this time. Learning relaxation breathing techniques or practicing meditation daily can help keep negative effects of stress to a minimum. If your care provider approves, taking warm bubble baths and lighting candles or incense in the bathroom can be a wonderful relaxing treat. (Tub baths are often discouraged as delivery time gets closer.)

HANDLING NAUSEA

Nausea is a common complaint for some during the first three months of pregnancy. Many health-care providers now prescribe a vitamin B_6 supplement and many pregnant women have reported positive results. Eating smaller meals more often also seems to help prevent this unpleasant part of pregnancy. Certain herbal teas, such as chamomile mixed with a little ginger, can often help relieve this discomfort but be careful to avoid the herb teas that can be irritating and even dangerous if ingested in large quantities. Check with your health-care provider and do some reading to learn more about the wonders and safety of herbs. Susun Weed's book, *The Wise Woman Herbal for the Childbearing Years* is a wonderful resource (see bibliography).

In summary, baby becomes what mother does or does not eat. More nutrients are needed during pregnancy and lactation—especially protein, calcium, iron, folic acid and D and B vitamins—than at any other time in life. Eating well is a great way to show love for baby right from the start. A healthy mom is a nice present too!

Chapter Five

INFANT NUTRITION

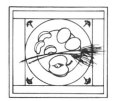

N utrition involves your body's use of the food you eat.
This simple statement helps remind parents of the important responsibility of choosing foods for their baby. No two babies have the exact same nutritional requirements. Age, gender, weight, physical activity, medical conditions, climate and environment all must be considered to determine specific dietary needs.

It's difficult to sort out accurate information about nutrition these days. Each new study often contradicts the one before it. When doing research on nutrition, I have looked for studies conducted by scientists who were not associated with or paid by large food corporations or associations (such as the American Dairy or Cattle Association). It's amazing to read the results of studies funded by food companies that indicate their own products are nutritious and safe.

Current news articles about nutrition elicit many questions. Do antioxidants (such as vitamins C and E) actually prevent cancer? Is sugar that harmful? And what's the truth about vitamin and herbal supplements? Is butter or margarine better now that we know about transfats? Should we give whole milk or skim milk to toddlers, or any milk at all? Different groups have come up with different answers to all of these questions. New studies will show us that this food substance can lead to cancer and that wonder food prevents cancer (this month). Various interest groups, both government and private, all have their own data to support various claims.

As I did in the first edition of this book, I filtered through this information as best I could from my background and experiences as a professional health educator and mother. I continue to look at the big picture of nutrition and I am always wary of extremes. I also continue to maintain that *balance* and a healthy attitude are essential in making food choices. Consuming too much of any food or supplement could be detrimental. Eating a variety of wholesome, unprocessed, organically grown (if possible) foods in a relaxed and peaceful setting and getting adequate exercise make the most sense to me when it comes to healthy nutrition and diet. Your own common sense, thoughtful decision making and consulting with your health-care provider for special dietary needs is probably your best guide.

DEFINING VEGETARIANS

A few definitions are in order before going any further. There are several different "categories" of vegetarians. The use of the word "vegetarian" in this book means a diet that contains no meat, but includes dairy products and eggs. One choosing these foods is known as a *lacto-ovo vegetarian*. Some people in this category occasionally include poultry or fish in their diet as well.

Another kind of vegetarian is called a *vegan*. Vegans obtain their protein from plant sources only and do not eat any dairy products. A *note of caution*: one following this type of diet must take a vitamin B_{12} supplement, because this essential vitamin is scarce in the vegan's food selection.

Another type of vegetarian is the *lacto-vegetarian*. This person eats dairy products but no eggs (and of course no meats).

A note of caution to people (often teenagers) who want to be vegetarians, but may not understand the importance of choosing proper protein foods for their diet. If a person sits down to a meal with meat, potatoes and vegetables on the table and simply avoids the meat, protein requirements will not be met. Worse yet is the choice of an entirely meatless but highly processed diet. If you know a "vegetarian" in this category, please share information with them about protein complementarity (defined below) and the importance of eating a variety of unprocessed, whole foods.

FOOD GROUPS

As parents begin the process of planning wholesome meals and making baby's food, a quick review of nutrition is in order. Instant recall of what foods have which vitamins is not necessary, but an overall picture of a few basics will help.

Take a quick look at the food charts on pages 36-43. Included are four different charts:

Food Pyramid
Vegetarian Four Food Groups
New Four Food Groups
Allergy Basic Four Food Groups

These food charts take on more importance as we begin to menu plan for baby. (Remember that the serving size will be smaller for infants, larger for adults, and a bit larger for pregnant or lactating women and teens.) Choose the one (or two) needed for your family, put a copy on your refrigerator door and organizing meals should be a bit easier. You now are one step closer to ensuring your baby is fed well.

Food Pyramid

The old basic four food groups many of us learned about in high school health class have been replaced by the new Food Pyramid (see pages 36-37). This pyramid represents the latest research from the United States Department of Agriculture (USDA) and is a guide to choosing foods necessary to obtain optimum nutrients, minimum fat and the right amount of calories to maintain a healthy weight. These guidelines are recommended for Americans over the age of two and do include meat, poultry and fish in a food group along with dry beans, eggs and nuts. The USDA advocates eating a variety of foods from each of the parts of the pyramid, with more servings from the base and fewer from the tip of the pyramid.

Vegetarian Four Food Groups

If a diet does not include meat, fish or poultry, the Vegetarian Four Food Groups (see pages 38-39) serves as a more accurate guide than the Food Pyramid. Note the major difference between the Vegetarian Four Food Groups chart and the Food Pyramid. A person on a lacto-ovo vegetarian diet should choose six daily servings from the grain-legumes-nut-seeds group rather than three servings from the section that contains meat, poultry and fish. Eggs are listed as a food source in the dairy section of the lacto-ovo vegetarian chart.

New Four Food Groups

In 1991 the Physicians Committee for Responsible Medicine (PCRM) developed and recommended the New Four Food Group

Guidelines for vegans (who eat no meat, fish, poultry, eggs or dairy products). The PCRM (doctors and laypersons working together for compassionate and effective medical practice, research and health promotion) strongly advocates vegan diets as the "healthiest of all." Their low-fat, no-cholesterol plan emphasizes foods from the plant kingdom as its protein and calcium source. This well-researched food plan includes the daily nutritional requirement for an average adult. PCRM is quick to remind vegans to be certain they consume enough foods with B_{12}, foods fortified with B_{12}, or take a good multivitamin supplement that contains this crucial vitamin. Tempeh, a good source of B_{12}, is listed in the "legume" food group. PCRM produces an excellent booklet called the *Vegetarian Starter Kit* (listed in the bibliography) that provides an excellent overview of this healthy diet, including a few recipes. See page 40 for the New Four Food Groups chart.

Allergy Basic Four Food Groups

The Allergy Basic Four Food Groups chart (see page 42) is a guide for substituting different foods for those containing milk, eggs, wheat or corn. All four are common causes of food allergy. You will note that nonmilk products replace foods found in the Pyramid milk, yogurt and cheese group. If your child is allergic to wheat or corn, adaptations can be made when selecting foods from the grain group.

If you decide to feed your child a vegetarian diet, or are changing to a meat-free diet yourself, a properly planned menu will assure enough protein. The first few times your baby has three meals a day, you might want to chart the items eaten under the various groups. This may help in your menu-planning and ensure that your baby is eating foods from the various food groups.

PROTEIN COMPLEMENTARITY

The rapid cell growth in the brain (and entire body) during early life makes it essential for baby to have enough protein to achieve optimum development. The best way to obtain protein without eating meat is to combine certain incomplete proteins. The proper combining of various protein foods is known as *protein complementarity*. Proper combinations of these foods eaten during the same meal or even within several hours can ensure that your child obtains the same amount of protein contained in meat or eggs.

When the first edition of *Into the Mouths of Babes* was published in 1984, it was thought essential to combine certain protein foods in the same meal in order to achieve complementarity and optimal benefits from the protein. The latest research indicates that we can eat complementary protein within three to four hours and still meet the required protein requirements. In other words, we don't need to combine proteins at each meal, if we eat more frequent smaller meals with various sources of plant protein.

Animal products, fish and soybeans have all eight of the essential amino acids necessary to form protein for use in our body. Because these amino acids are in "ready-to-use" form, many people tend to think of milk and eggs as perfect protein foods. Fortunately, it has been discovered that other foods are made up of incomplete plant proteins: legumes, dried peas and beans, dairy products, grains, nuts and seeds. The proper combination of any of these food groups forms a complete protein. A few examples of dishes containing complementary proteins include: rice and bean casserole, corn tortillas and beans, whole grain cereals and milk, falafel (garbanzo beans with sesame seeds in a mixture), whole wheat pizza (whole wheat and cheese), enchilada bake (corn, beans and cheese), lentil soup topped with cheese, and peanut butter balls (peanuts and nonfat dry milk). These dishes are economical and baby has an easier time with digestion.

See the chart on page 43 for suggestions on food combinations that form complete proteins. For more information about protein complementarity, the most recent edition of *Diet for a Small Planet: Twentieth Anniversary Edition*, by Frances Moore Lappe, is an excellent source.

NUTRIENTS

Along with knowledge of various food groups, we need to take a look at the kinds of nutrients needed for baby's energy, growth and development.

Your baby will grow faster during the first year than at any other time in life. A healthy, growing baby needs the same number of nutrients as an adult but in lesser amounts. There are over forty-five nutrients divided into six classifications:

Protein
Carbohydrates
Fats and oils
Vitamins
Minerals
Water

PROTEIN

Protein is essential for the rapid growth, development and repair of all body tissues (muscles, blood, glands, heart, brain, nerves and skin). Next to water, it makes up the largest portion (approximately 15-20 percent) of body weight. Protein is also needed for the formation of enzymes (to aid digestion), hormones (to regulate many body functions) and antibodies (to counteract foreign substances that can cause illness). Inadequate protein can retard growth and can also lower resistance to disease and infections. Since protein is not stored by the body, baby needs adequate amounts of protein each day.

CARBOHYDRATES

Carbohydrates are known to us in the forms of sugar, starch and cellulose. They provide baby with most of the total calories needed for heat and energy. As the major source of immediate energy and also the energy source for the brain and nervous system, carbohydrates obviously are important to baby's diet. They aid the body in the use of protein and fat and many carbohydrates will end up being stored in the body as fat. If the carbohydrate intake is too low, the body must use what little it gets for fuel rather than for growth. Cellulose is the indigestible carbohydrate found in many vegetables and fruits. Carbohydrates should make up about 60 percent of baby's diet and should be eaten in the least refined form for optimum benefit.

Natural Starch Sources

Bananas	Pasta
Cereals	Peas
Corn	Potatoes
Dried peas and beans	Winter squash

Natural Sugar Sources

Apples	Oranges
Bananas	Peas
Carrots	Honey
Grapes	

FATS AND OILS

We've all heard the bad news about fats. Studies have linked high-fat diets to heart disease, cancer and other illnesses. Fatty foods contribute to obesity and calories consumed through fat don't leave as much room for grains, fruits and vegetables. Most nutritionists recommend that we limit our fat intake to 30 percent of our calories and that we should consume most of these calories through unsaturated fats (olive, avocado, peanut, canola, corn, safflower, sesame oils). Other experts think 30 percent is still too much fat. Dean Ornish, MD, the renowned physician who developed a plan to reverse heart disease, advises that we consume no more than 10 to 15 percent of our total calories through fat. The National Research Council's recommendations to prevent cancer include suggestions that we consume less fat (30 percent or less of the total calories) in our daily diets, and to be sure to eat fresh vegetables, fruits and whole grains daily.

But there is good news about fat too. Fats and oils are needed to ensure good use of proteins and carbohydrates. They also provide the body with a reserve energy supply. Without enough fat in the diet, baby would need to burn up protein for energy. Fats help to delay hunger, add flavor to foods, help maintain healthy skin and hair and aid in the absorption of the fat-soluble vitamins (A, D, E and K). Stored fats are essential in maintaining a constant body temperature, and they help protect the internal organs from injury. Many American diets have traditionally been high in fats. Most fast-food restaurants and quick convenient foods are noted for their high fat content. Being sure to choose wholesome, natural foods and being conscious of how they are prepared helps reduce the worry about a diet too high in fats.

The essential fatty acids found in fats and oils are important for baby's growth and for maintaining healthy skin. Essential fatty acids are: linoleic acid, linolenic acid and arachidonic acid. Of these three, linoleic acid is most important.

Good sources of linoleic acid

Breast milk	Safflower oil
Avocados	Sesame oil
Soybeans	Sunflower oil
Sunflower seeds	Soy oil
Sesame seeds	

Baby can get fats and oils needed from natural foods such as:

Low-fat dairy products	Peanut butter
Grains	Sesame seeds (ground)
Avocados	Sunflower seeds (ground)
Soybeans	

VITAMINS

The delicate balance between health and disease often is dependent on what vitamins are consumed and used properly by our bodies. Vitamins, in their natural state, are small organic substances found in foods and are necessary for life. Babies eating a variety of natural foods usually have little problem getting enough vitamins.

Natural vitamin supplements are usually preferred over synthetic vitamins. Synthetic vitamins and natural vitamins have the same chemical analysis. However, a synthetically derived vitamin can cause toxic reactions in some susceptible people while the same vitamin in natural form is tolerated. Some authorities believe there are fewer gastrointestinal upsets with natural vitamin supplements.

Authorities differ on the necessity of vitamin supplements. Some say that if one eats a proper diet, there is no additional need for vitamins. Others, while encouraging a good diet, believe various factors (stress, disease, smoking, medications) cause more vitamins to be used by the body and leave people with a detrimental shortage of vitamins. Eating processed foods poor in vitamins also can cause various deficiencies.

Authorities also disagree on the need to regulate vitamins, minerals and other supplements. The early 1990s found the vitamin industry at odds with the Food and Drug Administration, which has advocated tighter control of these products under the argument of consumer protection. Hopefully, a workable solution to this problem will protect consumers from fraudulent claims while maintaining easy access to these products.

Although all the nutrients humans need can be obtained by eating a good balance of whole and natural foods, it must be mentioned that foods grown in today's soil are not as rich in vitamins and other nutrients as they were a hundred years ago. Increased pollution of air, soil and water has caused food sources to be more contaminated than in the past. Therefore, vitamin supplements, taken properly and with good meals and under medical supervision, can ensure a healthy level of vitamins in the body.

Name That Vitamin

There are two types of vitamins: water soluble (B complex and C) and fat soluble (A, D, E and K). Water-soluble vitamins are not stored in the body and, therefore, need to be replaced daily.

The fat-soluble vitamins are stored in the body. They cannot be found in harmful amounts in the foods we eat. However, if too many vitamin supplements of A, D, E and K are taken, they can cause problems. For example, an overdose of vitamin A can result in nausea, vomiting, bone pain, hair loss, blurred vision, rashes, fatigue and/or liver enlargement. Excessive vitamin D can cause too much calcium to be absorbed and removed from bones, resulting in damage to the heart, lungs and blood vessels. Nausea, vomiting, dizziness and diarrhea can also occur if large amounts are taken too suddenly.

Remember, vitamins are not substitutes for foods, nor are they pep pills. They have no caloric or energy value of their own. If vitamins are consumed without proper diet, good health will disappear.

Vitamin A
(fat-soluble)
Functions: Necessary for growth, good eyesight, strong bones, healthy skin, teeth, gums and hair. Helps baby to build resistance against respiratory infections. Good sources:

Carrots	Milk
Eggs	Dairy products
Fish liver oil	Breast milk
Green and yellow vegetables	Liver
Yellow fruits	Kidney

Vitamin B Complex
(water-soluble)
Functions: Allows body to obtain energy from carbohydrates. Promotes growth, healthy appetite and skin, and aids in digestive process. Essential for keeping good balance in nervous system. Good sources:

Brewer's yeast	Leafy green vegetables
Wheat germ	Breast milk
Wheat bran	Milk
Nuts	Brown rice
Dried beans and peas	Cheese
Soybeans	Egg yolk
Pork	Bananas
Organ meats	Lentils
Fish	Peanut butter
Poultry	

Vitamin C
(water-soluble)

Functions: Needed by the body cells for growth, repair of body tissues, strong bones, teeth, gums and blood vessels. Helps body absorb iron. Good sources:

Citrus fruits	Potatoes
Green and leafy vegetables	Sweet potatoes
Breast milk	Tomatoes

Vitamin D
(the fat-soluble sunshine vitamin)

Functions: Essential to baby's bone formation by providing proper utilization of calcium and phosphorus. Important for good teeth. Good sources:

Sunlight	Salmon
Milk	Tuna
Dairy products	Herring
Fish liver oils	Sardines

Vitamin E
(fat-soluble)

Functions: Necessary for cellular growth, helping promote endurance and alleviating fatigue. Provides protection against air pollution and is especially helpful for babies. Good sources:

Breast milk	Brussels sprouts
Wheat germ oil	Leafy greens
Peanut oil	Spinach
Soy oil	Nuts
Whole grains	Eggs
Wheat germ	

Vitamin K
(fat-soluble)

Function: Essential for proper clotting of blood; i.e., allowing tissue to form over cuts and scrapes. Good sources:

Breast milk
Alfalfa
Yogurt
Egg yolk
Safflower oil

Soybean oil
Leafy green vegetables
Cauliflower
Kelp
Cabbage

MINERALS

Minerals are elements contained in each cell in your body. Although minerals comprise only 4 percent of the body's weight, they are an extremely important nutrient because they are essential to regulating many vital bodily functions such as bone formation and the action of the heart and digestive system.

There are over sixty minerals in the body, but only twenty-two are considered essential. Seven of these minerals — calcium, chlorine, magnesium, phosphorus, potassium, sodium and sulfur — are present in large quantities. The other essential minerals are present in such small quantities that they are referred to as "trace" minerals. These trace minerals are also essential for your baby's growth:

Boron
Chromium (chloride)
Copper
Fluorine (fluoride)
Iodine

Iron
Manganese
Molybdenum
Selenium
Zinc

Calcium, iron and sodium are three key minerals we should know about. Sodium (usually through salt) is typically consumed in excess in many of our diets. Calcium and iron, on the other hand, are often found in low amounts in the average diet.

Calcium

Function: More calcium is in the body than any other mineral (most of it can be found in the bones and teeth in an adult). Important for health, formation of bones and teeth. Good sources:

Cheese
Dried beans
Green vegetables
Peanuts
Salmon

Sardines
Sesame seeds
Soybeans
Sunflower seeds
Walnuts

Iron
Function: Essential for blood formation. Good sources:

Leafy green vegetables   Peas
Pasta   Eggs
Bread   Liver
Dried fruits   Kidneys
Nuts   Meat, poultry, fish
Beans

Sodium
Functions: Essential for normal growth; works with potassium to regulate the amount of water in and around body cells. Helps nerves and muscles to function properly. Good sources:

Salt   Dried beef
Beets   Brains
Carrots   Kidney
Artichokes   Shellfish
Bacon

Phosphorus
Function: Properly balanced with calcium it helps bone and teeth formation and helps muscle, nerve and kidney function. Good sources:

Whole grains   Fish
Eggs   Poultry
Nuts   Meat
Seeds   Red cabbage

Potassium
Functions: Works with sodium to regulate proper water balance in the body. Helps regulate blood flow to make the heart pump efficiently, and works with magnesium in synthesizing protein. Combines with phosphorus to send oxygen to the brain. Good sources:

Bananas   Sunflower seeds
Citrus fruits   Potatoes
Dried beans   Mint leaves
Green leafy vegetables

Magnesium

Functions: Necessary for efficient nerve and muscle functions, strong bones and teeth, and allowing the enzymes in the body to work properly. Good sources:

Almonds	Apples
Figs	Lemons
Nuts	Seeds
Dark green vegetables	Yellow corn
Dried beans and peas	Whole grains

WATER

Water is the most important nutrient (although authorities often differ as to whether or not water is a nutrient). Because of its obvious importance to the body tissues and functions, it is included here. At least one-half of the body's weight actually is water. The human body cannot live longer than a few days without this important nutrient.

Babies get most of their water from drinking water and fruit juices, and eating fruits and vegetables. This water is necessary for digestion, removing body wastes and regulating body temperature.

Babies lose water daily through urine (confirmed by the neverending diaper changes), bowel movements (lots of those, too) and also through perspiration. Vomiting and diarrhea also cause water loss. Dehydration can occur in infants more readily than in adults, so be sure baby's liquid intake is adequate. Most authorities suggest a guideline of one-third cup liquid be given for each pound of the baby's weight until the total reaches six cups per day.

A breast-fed baby gets plenty of water through mother's milk, according to Karen Pryor in *Nursing Your Baby*. She suggests the mother should drink more water during hot weather, not the baby. An occasional bottle of water can be given during the first six months of nursing when juices have not yet been introduced but a nursing baby really obtains enough water through breast milk. Formula-fed babies need bottles of water to help the kidneys in eliminating the proteins and salts, found in cow's milk, which are not used by the human body.

Food Pyramid
(for diets that include meat)

Food Group	Servings	Food Sources
Fats, Oils and Sweets	Use sparingly	salad dressings, oils, cream, butter, sugars, margarine, candies, soft drinks, sweet desserts
Meat, Poultry, Fish, Dry Beans, Eggs and Nuts	2-3	beef, poultry, fish, dry beans, eggs, nuts
Milk, Yogurt and Cheese	2-3	milk, yogurt, cheese
Fruits	2-4	Citrus fruits: oranges, grapefruits, tangerines, lemons, pineapples Sweet fruits: peaches, pears, grapes, apricots, bananas, avocados, apples
Vegetables	3-5	Choose from dark green, leafy or other vegetables: green beans, peas, zucchini, broccoli, spinach, kale, carrots, lettuce, cabbage, squash, corn, cauliflower, potatoes
Bread, Cereal, Rice and Pasta	6-11	breads, cereals, rice, pasta

The Food Pyramid emphasizes foods from the five major food groups shown in the three lower sections of the pyramid on the opposite page. The small tip of the pyramid on the opposite page shows fats, oils and sweets, which are *not* a food group. These foods provide calories and little else of nutritional value. Most people should use them sparingly. (Adapted from the USDA Food Guide Pyramid.)

Food Pyramid

Vegetarian Four Food Groups
(for lacto-ovo vegetarian diets)

Food Group	Servings	Food Sources	
Dairy	3	milk cheese eggs yogurt	
Fruits	1-4	**Citrus** oranges lemons limes grapefruits tangerines pineapples	**Sweet** peaches pears apricots grapes bananas avocados apples
Vegetables	3	green beans peas green pepper zucchini broccoli spinach kale lettuce	cabbage carrots squash pumpkin corn tomatoes cauliflower potatoes
Grains	6	**Grains:** rice, oats, rye, millet, barley, corn **Legumes:** garbanzo beans, dried beans, dried peas, lentils **Nuts:** peanuts, almonds, walnuts **Seeds:** sesame, sunflower	

Vegetarian Four Food Groups

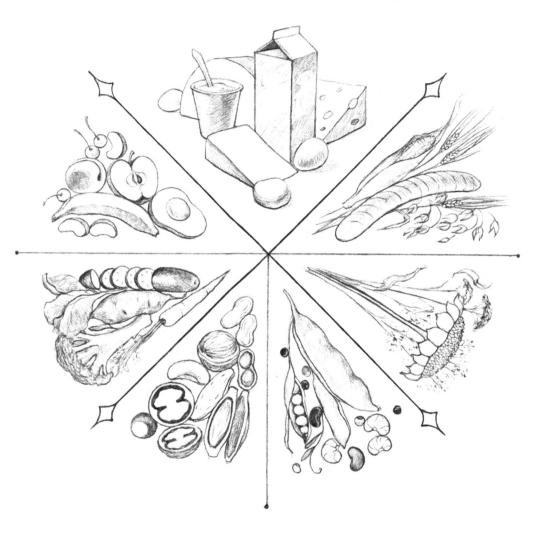

New Four Food Groups*
(for vegans)

Food Group	Servings	Food Sources
Vegetables	3 or more	broccoli, collards, kale, mustard and turnip greens, chicory, bok choy, carrots, winter squash, sweet potatoes, pumpkin
Whole Grains	5 or more	bread, rice, pasta, hot or cold cereal, millet, corn, barley, bulgur, buckwheat, groats, tortillas
Fruit	3 or more	Choose from any citrus, sweet fruit, melons and berries. Be sure to include at least 1 serving each day of fruits high in vitamin C—citrus fruits, melons, strawberries are good choices.
Legumes	2 or more	beans, peas, lentils, soy milk, tempeh, tofu

*Used with permission from the Physicians Committee for Responsible Medicine

New Four Food Groups

Allergy Basic Four Food Groups
(for those with food allergies)

Food Group	Servings	Food Sources
Dairy	3	(Milk-free or egg-free diet) milk-free formula, soy milk, nut milk (as recommended by physician)
Fruits and Vegetables	4	any fruit or vegetable not causing allergic reactions (watch out for citrus fruits)
Meat/ Protein	2	meat fish poultry (as recommended by physician)
Grains	4	(Wheat-free or corn-free diet) rice, millet, arrowroot, oats, rice flour, oat flour, barley flour, potato flour, rye flour, soy flour

Food Combinations That Form Complete Proteins

	Corn	Beans/legumes	Milk	Peanuts	Potatoes	Rice	Sesame seeds	Soybeans	Sunflower seeds	Wheat
Beans or legumes	•		•			•	•			•
Corn		•								
Corn & milk								•		
Corn & soy			•							
Milk		•		•	•	•	•			•
Milk & peanuts										•
Peanuts			•						•	
Peanuts & sesame seeds								•		
Rice	•	•								
Rice & wheat								•		
Sesame seeds	•	•								
Sesame seeds & soy				•						•
Sesame seeds & wheat								•		
Sunflower seeds				•						
Wheat	•	•								
Wheat & milk				•						
Wheat & peanuts			•							
Wheat & soy							•			

Chapter Six

FEEDING YOUR BABY

To breast-feed or not to breast-feed, that is the first question to be answered! This choice ultimately is made by the mother after considering the advantages and disadvantages of breast-feeding and bottle-feeding while keeping in mind her present life-style.

The decision to breast-feed or formula-feed your baby should be given a lot of thought. If you are uncertain as to which way you want to go, do some thorough research. Read some of the books listed in the bibliography and discuss both options with your mate and health-care provider.

THE BREAST-FEEDING ADVANTAGE

The awesome experience of nursing both of our children makes me lean toward encouraging all mothers to at least try breast-feeding. Breast-feeding can provide a special bond between mother and child, creating an inner peace and intense joy that is wonderfully overwhelming.

However, the choice to breast-feed is made knowing that the mother must always (or almost always) be available for the infant. Many mothers use a breast pump to save their own milk and freeze it for use when they are not available at feeding time. Karen Pryor's book, *Nursing Your Baby*, provides valuable information for any woman who is considering breast-feeding. The La Leche League in your area is a very helpful support group available for additional information.

It is very important for the nursing mother to maintain a good diet to ensure optimum nutritional benefits from her milk. If the mother eats a well-balanced diet, she will pass on to baby adequate amounts of essential vitamins. A nursing mother expends approximately 1,000 calories per day while nursing her baby. This factor is often helpful in regaining or improving on the prepregnancy weight of the mother. (Be careful not to skimp on nutritional needs at this time though!)

Breast-feeding also brings with it certain responsibilities and time constraints. The decision to breast-feed is made knowing that the mother must be readily available for her baby. Many women who return to work outside the home after the baby's birth may choose to combine breast- and bottle-feeding, pump breast milk during the work day, or choose bottle-feeding instead. A breast-feeding mother must also make sure her diet is one of quality, to provide her and the baby with necessary nutrients.

In rare instances, some mothers (an estimated 5 percent) do not produce enough milk and a dangerous condition known as *low-milk syndrome* can occur. This condition causes severe dehydration in infants which can result in strokes, blood clots or seizures. One warning sign occurs during the first several months of pregnancy if there is no significant swelling of the breasts. If baby is getting enough breast milk, it will be evident in the diaper changes. In the early weeks of life, a breast fed baby should have frequent bowel movements and at least six wet diapers each day.

Since many mothers are now leaving the hospital within a day or two of the birth, some pediatricians are beginning to recommend a checkup for babies when they are three or four days old. Don't hesitate to call the pediatrician if you have any concerns about your baby getting enough nourishment.

Making the decision to breast-feed also can bring with it the disapproval of parents, friends or relatives who may not be as comfortable as you are with this way of feeding. Fortunately, the recent increase in the number of nursing mothers has helped in the acceptance of this time-honored method of feeding.

Many parents have found that a combination of formula-feeding and breast-feeding works best for them. It gives their mate a special time to be with the baby at mealtime and frees the mother for a more flexible schedule.

HINTS FOR BOTTLE-FEEDING

If the decision is made to bottle-feed—for whatever reason—don't let any nursing mothers (or anyone) make you feel uncomfortable with your

Note: Most authorities suggest waiting to make the switch from bottle or breast to whole milk until age one. For this reason, formula or breast milk is used in all the recipes for babies under age one.

decision. Part of their enthusiasm for nursing often spills over into a religious-type fervor that prompts them to "spread the word" as to how wonderful breast-feeding is for everyone. It isn't wonderful for everyone in every situation! Certain medical situations and life situations may eliminate breast-feeding as an option. Make a realistic decision as to what is best for *you.*

If you decide to bottle-feed, be sure to choose an iron-fortified formula. It is essential that all bottles, nipples and utensils are clean. These are other helpful hints for parents who are feeding their baby formula:

- Make a one-day supply of formula at a time and throw away unused formula at the end of the day.
- If you choose a ready-to-drink formula, do not add any water. (This type is more expensive, but convenient for traveling.)
- Never force baby to finish a bottle. Heed the baby's signals when he attempts to "tell" you he is finished.
- Never prop a bottle — this could cause choking. Holding your baby close helps make feeding times a warmer experience for baby and the person feeding him.
- Follow the pediatrician's advice as to how much formula to give your baby.
- Be sure to ask the health care provider for proper vitamin supplements during these early feeding times.

BREAST-FEEDING
Advantages

Mother-infant bonding is very strong

Breast milk is nature's most perfect food

Said to aid in preventing certain allergies and decreasing chances of ear infection

Said to give some protection against disease

Helps uterus shrink faster

More economical

Baby's need to suck is naturally satisfied

Timesaving—time is not needed to prepare formula or clean bottles
Easy to travel with a nursing baby
Milk is always available if mother eats properly
Milk is always the proper temperature
No formula stain on baby's clothing
Infant utilizes the protein in the breast milk with maximum efficiency
Little danger of baby being overfed
Baby's stools do not have an unpleasant odor

Disadvantages

Mother must be available at feeding time
Other family members have little part in feeding milk
Possibility of negative attitude from family and friends
Cannot easily leave baby for prolonged amount of time

BOTTLE-FEEDING
Advantages

More convenient in some ways because baby can be fed a bottle by
    anyone, not just the mother
Frees the mother if time is needed away from home
Other family members can have more involvement with feedings

Disadvantages

Time needed to sterilize and prepare bottles
Odor of baby's stool is strong and unpleasant
Possibility of overfeeding
Propped bottles of milk can lead to tooth decay

THAT BIG DAY . . . STARTING SOLIDS!

As your baby approaches his six-month birthday, he will begin to show
signs that milk is not enough to satisfy his hunger. When his appetite
noticeably increases or when he begins to reach for food at the family
table, these are good indications that your baby is ready to start solid
foods. Current recommendations on starting solids suggest you wait
until the baby is six months old. This philosophy is reflected in this
book. (See chart that begins on page 56.)

Once a baby starts on a solid diet, the parents (and other caregivers)
have the task of choosing the foods that will supply baby with essential

vitamins and minerals. Since there are many differing views on the necessity for vitamin supplements, consult your child's health-care provider before making your decision.

By six months of age the iron supply a baby is born with will almost be depleted, so it is important to make sure iron is included in your baby's diet. Because cereal is a good source of iron, it often is the first "solid" food to be introduced. Choose a rice or oat cereal; wait to give any wheat cereal until eight months or so because many babies will have an allergic reaction if this food is introduced too early.

First Feedings

The first feeding should be just a spoonful or two (try to avoid the urge to make enough for all the kids on the block!), offered gently, for the baby to experiment with the new sensation. This will be an entirely new experience for your baby so try not to rush things. Baby can be fed from a small baby chair, on your lap, or securely and comfortably in a high chair. It doesn't matter whether the cereal is offered for breakfast or lunch, but it probably is best to choose a nonfussy time of day when baby is contented.

Offer the same food all week, gradually increasing the amount to about three to four tablespoons. The next week, offer another cereal or a fruit. Mashed ripe banana is a real favorite, with a nice taste that most babies will enjoy. The amount of food served will vary from baby to baby and slowly increase with age. Use your good judgment and let your baby help to guide you. Babies' instincts are very interesting! They usually know when they are hungry and when to stop eating.

Soon banana and rice cereal can be combined for a meal, or you can offer cereal for breakfast and banana for lunch. Juice can be introduced for snack time but be careful not to replace the nutrients and calories baby needs by giving him too much juice. A recent study published in the *Pediatrics* journal indicated that malnutrition resulted when infants consumed large quantities of juice, which left them with little appetite for food. Try offering juice occasionally in a small spouted cup rather than in a bottle. Babies catch on quickly and it will reduce the amount they drink. Diluted apple juice or strained orange juice usually is well liked. Don't buy the baby food juices unless you don't mind the extra cost. Check labels on the apple juice, and choose a juice made of apples and water and nothing else. Choose a frozen orange juice with nothing extra added, or fresh squeeze the juice through a strainer; this will catch the strands of pulp that often make a baby gag.

INTRODUCING NEW FOODS

Gradually introduce a variety of fruits and cereals over a two-month period. Avocados, cooked apples, pears, peaches, papaya and apricots are good fruits to choose. Check the recipe section for preparation.

All foods should be pureed and portions kept small. Start with one meal a day the first few weeks, then gradually go to two meals. Keep in mind your child's individual needs, and watch for signs of hunger or overfeeding. It is especially important to only offer one new food per week. If any allergic reaction should occur (rash, diarrhea or irritability), it is more easily pinpointed when foods are offered in this manner.

Yogurt

Whole-milk yogurt is an excellent food to offer at around six or seven months. Yogurt is a nutritious food highly noted for its abundance of B vitamins and for its beneficial effects to the digestive system. It is interesting to note that this whole-milk product is usually tolerated very well at this age, although whole milk itself is not recommended for a baby before age one. The reason is this: the fermenting process of the milk breaks down the lactose (milk sugar) into lactic acid. Therefore, that step in the digestive process is already completed by the time it reaches the stomach, making yogurt more acceptable to a baby with a milk intolerance. A milk intolerance can cause abdominal discomfort, bloating, diarrhea and gas. If you suspect your child has a milk *allergy* (rather than a milk intolerance), yogurt should *not* be given (see page 61 for symptoms of allergy). When in doubt about a suspected milk allergy or intolerance, get advice from your health-care provider.

You might want to invest in a yogurt maker or borrow one from a friend. You can make five containers of yogurt with very little time, effort or expense. All you need (in addition to the yogurt maker) is four cups of milk and one tablespoon of whole milk yogurt. It's worth checking into if you think you would eat the yogurt.

Vegetables

At around seven months, vegetables can be introduced (one a week, of course). It is easy to prepare larger batches of carrots, beans, peas or squash and freeze them for easy use later. Fresh, cooked vegetables will have the maximum amount of vitamins and minerals, so it's easy to give baby a portion of fresh vegetables any time the family is eating them.

Just puree them in the blender or baby food grinder. More grain cereals also can be introduced at around seven months of age. Try millet or barley cereal.

At Eight to Nine Months

At eight months, baby begins to see a lot of options. Cooked egg yolk is good to offer at this time. Natural cheeses (avoid artificially made or colored cheeses) are usually loved by the eight-month-old. Stronger vegetables such as cabbage, broccoli and spinach can be pureed for baby.

Nine months and a few teeth later, foods can be a bit lumpier, and the variety in the food groups broadens. Dried beans (garbanzo, lentils, pinto, soy, etc.) can be cooked, mashed and given to baby. Peanut butter can be mashed with banana and mixed with formula or breast milk. Be sure the mixture is very thin to prevent gagging. Bulgur, wheat cereal and more juices (grape, grapefruit, apricot) can be introduced. Tiny bite-size pieces of soft foods can be offered. Put newspaper or an old plastic tablecloth under the high chair, and don't worry about the mess your baby makes at this time. Many people get into the habit of never allowing their baby to feed himself or make a mess trying. This is what we're here for; one of our jobs is to let our babies have successes and failures! They'll never learn to eat until we let them try, slop and spill. I'm not advocating letting your two-year-old daughter finger paint on her tray with applesauce, but it is important that we give a nine-month-old the chance to reach his mouth. Give him a spoon, let him try.

Without sounding contradictory, it is important to remember that sometimes our children sense we are preparing them for great independence. They go through spells when they really prefer to have Mommy or Daddy shovel the food in for them. On this matter—indulge! They are just testing to see if we still will take that time with them. They seem sometimes to be saying they need that time. Someone once said, "They're only young once." So true.

A BASIC PHILOSOPHY OF FEEDING

Each of us has our likes and dislikes—and so do babies! By keeping this in mind and by making mealtimes as relaxed as possible, our babies will enjoy feeding times and so will you.

Never force your baby (or older child) to eat a certain food or even a certain amount of food. Babies are quite intelligent and instinctive about what they need to eat. As long as wholesome food is available for your baby to choose from, he will do just fine.

There are parents who hated the fact that they were forced to eat particular foods when they were little, but find themselves doing the same thing to their children. This cycle needs to be broken — for everyone's sake.

Babies' tastes will change. Just when you think Katie has formed a lifelong love affair with peas, the next day she'll refuse to eat them! Don't hassle. Don't panic. Quietly set them aside, and offer peas again a few days later.

Relax and enjoy baby's mealtime. Don't force your baby to eat. Respect your baby's tastes as you would have someone respect yours. Mealtimes will be a pleasure for everyone.

Influence of Grandparents

A word about grandparents. Just as we are learning to be good parents, many parents are working hard to be good grandparents. In their own way of trying to help us out, they often want to share their ideas on feeding, and are upset or bewildered that we may have chosen a "different" way to feed our baby. Breast-feeding is a great example. Many mothers who raised children during the fifties and sixties are appalled that someone would want to be bothered with breast-feeding. To many it is even embarrassing. If you have chosen to breast-feed, keep in mind that many mothers and grandmothers went through a great media blitz that convinced them formula was better than breast milk and much more convenient. They were told a good "modern" mother feeds her baby formula if she wants him to grow big and strong. Imagine the shock or surprise when her daughter or granddaughter chooses to refute all this and decides to breast-feed. "Are you sure he's getting enough to eat?" "How do you know how many ounces she drank?" "She's crying — see there, she's still hungry." Many a well-meaning grandparent has been known to utter these words. If you are truly comfortable and confident in your decision to breast-feed or to feed your baby a vegetarian diet, let all these comments go over your head. Getting angry or defensive doesn't help. A quiet, peaceful response to the questions will go much further to keep family peace.

This holds true for the type of food you choose to give your baby also. Prepackaged, processed, longer shelf-life foods were such wonderful new inventions in days past. And for many families, it wasn't a meal if meat wasn't on the table. Our parents chose to feed us the best way they knew how, just as we choose to feed our baby the most nutritious foods we can. There was little research done at that time concerning the ill effects of too much sugar, meat, fats, white flour and processed foods. So remember that our parents may, at first, feel a bit threatened by our knowledge of nutrition and our different ideas about baby food. A calm and frank discussion of how you made your decisions about feeding and how your parents (or friends) made theirs might ease any tension that has occurred. Also, a quiet "thank you" might be nice to parents who have given wholehearted support for the important decisions we are making on how we have chosen to feed our baby (thanks, Mom and Dad).

Maintaining Balance

A word here about "deviating" from an entirely natural, unprocessed, whole food diet. We try as hard as we can to plan, cook and provide healthy meals and snacks for our children. However, when our children were younger, we came to realize that we did not have total control over what went into the mouths of our babes day in and day out. While doing our best to have wholesome food in our kitchen, we learned not to get hysterical if our child had a cupcake or a piece of candy at a birthday party in school. Our belief is that if we make these foods "forbidden," we are setting our children up for failure. They cannot possibly comply with this expectation all the time. Therefore, we educated our children quietly on the topics of nutrition and protein sources, the hazards of sugar and processed food, and the differences between healthy food and food with little nutritional value. We allowed some "junk" food some of the time. (It was never offered as a reward for good behavior — that would not make sense if we told them to eat good food because we care about their health.) Those times were infrequent, and we tried hard to achieve a good balance in our daily diet. In other words, we believed a little bit of "nonperfect" food was not going to hurt in the overall view of things. However, if my child were hyperactive, diabetic, hypoglycemic or had some other suspected or diagnosed medical problem, those deviations from an excellent diet would be too risky and not worth the price the child would pay. As a parent, you need to make the choices and educate your child according to your life-style, culture and beliefs to provide balance in your family's life.

As the mother of two teenagers, I can look back and say that this philosophy worked well. Both Zac and Molly are *choosing* to be vegetarians, and both eat (for the most part) a variety of wholesome foods. They have reached for the veggie platter more than they reached for the junk food at parties. Although there is always room for improvement in their diets, I am proud of most of their food choices and their attitudes and knowledge about foods.

Avoid Overfeeding

Overfeeding an infant should not be considered a sign of our affection. With the creation of fat babies, we could also be creating fat adults. Those with weight problems would certainly wish they did not have the number of fat cells they've had since childhood. Fat cells created during infancy (and some authorities believe more develop during adolescence) are present in the same number that hold fat later in life. In other words, once fat cells develop, their numbers never decrease. The amount of fat stored in the body is determined by this number of fat cells.

Approximately 20 percent of American children are obese. The number of fat cells present in the bodies of these children will never disappear. Eating less food and getting more exercise can cause some of this fat to burn up (expend calories) and reduce the *size* of the fat cells, but the *number* of fat cells will remain stable, making it difficult to keep extra weight off.

Obesity is a numbers game, and the overweight children are the losers on the scale. Let's look at these numbers. An infant is born with 5 to 6 billion fat cells. These cells multiply to 30 to 40 billion by normal adulthood. Eating too much combined with little physical activity can cause fat cells to increase in number. Therefore, an obese adult, who was overweight as a child, might end up with 80 to 120 billion fat cells. Although these fat cells are of normal size, that is far too many of them. In contrast, if a person gains weight as an adult, the fat cells already in existence grow larger but the numbers stay constant. Overweight adults who were overweight children find it almost impossible to reduce their weight permanently.

As parents, we must do all we can to avoid overfeeding and underexercising our children. Don't put food in baby's mouth every time he or she cries. Let baby explore the world around him with you there for safety. Keep "confined time" to a minimum. Babies should not spend most of their day in a playpen or high chair. Remember that overfeeding is not a sign of love. Keep baby active and well fed but not *overfed*!

Establishing Good Habits

The overall selection of foods is important to keep in mind when menu-planning. Moderation, variety and the wholesomeness of the foods chosen should provide your child with optimum nutrition. Smith and Lifshitz in their *Pediatrics* journal article (see bibliography) wisely state, "Any single food consumed in excess, even if it is perceived as being healthful and nutritious, can result in dietary imbalance and affect the weight gain and growth of children."

Establishing good eating habits and good exercise habits at an early age will help our children get off to a good, healthy start in life. Exercise is important to all of us, but especially our young. It helps establish good habits for the future. Walk, run, swim, jump, skip, dance and stretch with your child. The rewards are endless!

Disordered Eating and Body Dissatisfaction

Early messages about food can lead to body dissatisfaction for our children. At one time children began to worry about their body image when they became teenagers, now many eight- and nine-year old children express disgust at their body image and studies show many have already tried dieting. Some of these children are well on their way to major eating disorders such as anorexia nervosa (starving and excessive weight loss), bulimia nervosa (binging food secretly followed by purging) and binge-eating (compulsive eating).

What does all this have to do with infant nutrition? Some of us learned many negative lessons about food when we were young. We may have learned to associate certain foods as being "bad." As adults we have heard, "Oh, that chocolate mousse looks sinful," and we have possibly felt guilty as we reached for a second helping of dessert. This has set many of us up for subconscious and conscious negative thinking about our food, weight and body image. These attitudes can be passed along to our children if we aren't careful.

And what has the media done to our negative thinking about body dissatisfaction? Plenty! Next time you're in the grocery store checkout line, scan the topics on the magazine covers. "Lose twelve pounds in two weeks," "Exercise for the perfect body," "He'll love you more after this diet," "Makeup tricks to make you look glamorous," or "Look thin in your swimsuit by following this surefire diet." In between these stories we see ten new dessert recipes, pages of picture-perfect models and then an article on how to increase our self-esteem. And the gorgeous face on the front cover beams up at us from a photograph altered with special effects that have made every pimple, flaw and pore disappear. Our self-esteem may take a nosedive before we unload the grocery cart!

Early messages from parents are often a repeat of what was said by their parents. "Eat all your carrots or you can't go out to play," "Don't eat too much ice cream, do you want to end up fat like your Aunt?" "You're a bad girl—you didn't eat everything on your plate," "If you don't eat all your broccoli you can't go to the movies." These messages, combined with what our children see on TV ("Use Thin Fast, I lost twelve pounds in two weeks," etc.) and the cultural norm that thin is in, is literally killing some of our children. Recent reports indicate that an estimated 10 percent of our high school and college students have eating disorders. Nine-year-old girls are already dieting seriously and many have some sort of disordered eating habits.

If you are reading this and the guilt is starting to creep in, throw your guilt out the window and keep reading. What we have experienced in the past has helped shape our present attitudes and beliefs about foods, but our past experience doesn't need to dictate our decisions for today or tomorrow. By learning to be sensitive to what we say to our children from this day forward, we can help lead them (and us) to a healthier life-style.

That First Year . . .
A Timetable* for Introducing Solid Foods

Food	6 months	7	8	9	10	11	12	Not until age 2
Apple juice	●							
Applesauce	●							
Avocado	●							
Banana	●							
Barley	●							
Beets		●						
Berries[1]								●
Broccoli			●					
Bulgur			●					
Cabbage			●					
Carrots		●						
Cottage cheese	●							
Cheese			●					
Egg white						●		
Egg yolk			●					
Green beans		●						
Honey[2] (uncooked)						●		
Legumes				●				
Milk (cow's)[3]						●		
Millet	●							
Nuts, seeds (whole)						●		
Oats (oatmeal)	●							
Orange juice						●		
Papaya	●							
Peaches		●						
Peanut butter			●					
Pears	●							

Food	6 months	7	8	9	10	11	12	Not until age 2
Peas		●						
Potato (mashed)			●					
Rice	●							
Spinach			●					
Sprouts (ground)			●					
Squash		●						
Sweet potato	●							
Tofu			●					
Tomato							●	
Yogurt	●							
Zucchini		●						

*This table contains information on suggested starting dates for various foods. Keep in mind that a baby should receive only one new food a week, and giving baby every food listed under each month is not recommended.

[1] Pureed berries can be offered gradually after 12 months. Whole berries still can cause gagging so be careful and consider how well your child chews his food. Some berries cause diaper rash or skin rashes, so just be aware.

[2] Uncooked honey has caused botulism and even death in children under age one. Do *not* feed infants uncooked honey before age one!

[3] Milk in this cookbook refers to breast milk or formula until age one. Authorities differ on starting dates for whole milk—some say it's okay at six months, and others suggest waiting until age one. I used milk in recipes that needed cooking or baking (i.e., pancakes, rice pudding, breads), after the age of seven months, but used breast milk (you can use formula) for drinking "straight." Follow the pediatrician's advice on when to start giving your child milk, and watch closely for any allergic symptoms or reactions. Many infants just cannot tolerate milk too early, and it would be a shame to put their little bodies through misery by neglecting to notice signs of sensitivity to milk.

Foods That Could Cause Problems

Food	Problem	Do Not Give to Baby Before Age:
Egg white	Allergy	1
Uncooked honey	Botulism, and possibly death, can occur in babies under a year old	1
Milk	Allergy	1
Wheat	Allergy	10-12 months
Whole Berries	Allergy, digestive problems	1½-2
Leafy vegetables	Gagging	1½-2
Peanut butter (not thinned)	Gagging	2
Popcorn	Choking	2
Whole nuts or seeds	Choking	3
Whole raisins	Choking	2
Whole corn	Gagging, choking	2
Chocolate	Allergy, digestive problems, too much sugar	3 (hold off as long as you can — they don't need it!)
Apple pieces, whole grapes	Choking	1
Candy, cookies	Choking	Over age 1 (hold off as long as you can!)
Carrot sticks	Choking	2

Note: This may be a good time to take a course in CPR and to learn how to deal with a baby or child who is choking.

Chapter Seven

COPING WITH FOOD ALLERGIES

The thousands of additives found in some of our foods today make it increasingly difficult to pinpoint specific food allergies. It seems the more we learn about allergies, the more complex the subject becomes.

Consider what many doctors and researchers have written about allergies. Food allergies and/or food intolerance:

- can occur at any age
- can appear after eating a food that has never caused an allergic reaction before
- can cause a reaction anywhere in the body
- cause symptoms to appear only after large amounts have been consumed
- can cause symptoms to appear only when foods are eaten during a certain season of the year
- can cause allergic reactions in one child in a family but not a sibling in the same family
- do not cause the same reaction all the time
- often occur in a variety of foods in the same food family

A few definitions are needed to help form a better picture of what happens to the body when subjected to an allergic food substance. A *food allergy* occurs when the body has an abnormal reaction after eating a particular food substance, causing one or more distressing symptoms to appear. An *allergen* is defined as something that causes an allergic reaction. Food, dust, mold, pollens and pets are common allergens. Our bodies react to these allergens by producing *antibodies*, which help to neutralize the action of the allergen. Food allergies appear when allergens enter the body with a certain food, and the body overproduces antibodies to counteract it.

The word allergy is derived from the Greek words allos, meaning "altered," and ergan, meaning "work" or "action." A food allergy causes an altered action, or intolerance, to take place in the body rather than a normal reaction.

CAUSES OF ALLERGY

Authorities have several theories as to just what causes an allergy. Heredity seems to be the biggest factor in most food allergies. Although it seems specific allergies are not transferred from parent to child, the tendency to react abnormally to various allergens can be transferred. Another possible cause of food allergy is overeating. Some bodies can only cope with a certain amount of an allergen; anything over this amount causes a reaction. There are doctors who believe certain stomach disturbances can cause food allergies.

What are the foods that can cause a food allergy? Any food can cause allergic reactions, but the most common foods are milk, wheat, corn, eggs, citrus, nuts, strawberries and shellfish. Cinnamon, chocolate and tomatoes also are high on the list of foods that cause problems. Foods containing artificial additives and dyes are frequent offenders as well.

The following foods are least likely to cause problems: rice, oats, barley, peaches, pears, bananas, applesauce, lettuce, carrots, grapes, squash and sweet potatoes. If one or both parents have a tendency toward allergies, these foods might help to ensure baby gets an allergy-free start when solid foods are introduced in the diet.

Doris Rapp, a well-known pediatric allergist, has written several books about allergies that are very helpful to the parent of an allergic child. In her book, *Allergies and Your Family*, Rapp includes a list of food additives frequently causing allergic responses. This list includes:

color additives	thickeners
flavorings	emulsifiers
antioxidants	pesticides
buffers	cod liver oil
preservatives	vitamins
stabilizers	minerals

This presents a rather gloomy situation for the parent who finds it necessary to constantly be reading labels at the supermarket.

In his book, *Earl Mindell's Food as Medicine*, Dr. Mindell compiled a list of what he believes are the twenty worst food additives. They are:

acacia gum (gum arabic)

alginic acid

aluminum

artificial color

benzaldehyde

benzoic acid

BHKA or BHT (butylated hydroxyanisole or butylated hydroxytoluene)

brominated vegetable oil

carrageenan

confectioner's glaze

EDTA (ethylenediaminetetraacetic acid-salts)

hydrolyzed vegetable protein (Mindell suggests this may cause brain or nervous system damage in infants)

iron salts (ferric pyrophosphate, ferric sodium pyrophosphate, ferrous lactate)

monoglycerides and diglycerides, acetylated monoglycerides and diglycerides

monosodium glutamate (MSG)

nitrates

paraffins (wax) [often found on fresh fruits and vegetables without food labels]

potassium bromate

propyl gallate (Dr. Mindell states this additive is banned from baby food or foods marketed to children in England, but it is not banned in the United States)

sulfites

ALLERGY SYMPTOMS

Symptoms of allergy can range from minor (itching skin or runny nose) to severe (convulsions or even death). Allergic symptoms can appear immediately after eating the offending food, or as long as several days afterward.

The most common symptoms of food allergy are:

itching
runny nose
swelling of lips
hives
mouth ulcers
headache
asthma
digestive problems (nausea, diarrhea, vomiting, gas)
irritability
fatigue
behavior problems

YEAST-RELATED COMPLEX

One allergic response creating problems in children (and adults) is caused by a yeast imbalance in the body. Yeast-Related Complex is connected with a certain pattern of medical complaints often undiagnosed. If your child acts or feels worse when it's damp and feels the same way when he eats yeast breads, ask your care provider about a possible connection between your child's poor health and a yeast imbalance. Rapp's book, *Is This Your Child?* (see bibliography), lists the medical complaints related to Yeast-Related Complex. Below are those specific to infants or children who may suffer from this illness:

white patches (thrush) inside the mouth
white-coated tongue
vaginal yeast infection or discharge
redness around the anus
diaper or other skin rashes
unpleasant odor to hair or feet
intestinal problems
hyperactivity
ear infections
nail abnormalities
bladder infections
genital touching
fatigue, lethargy or weakness
behavior problems
hives
insomnia
asthma

This is *not* an attempt to assume or diagnose a medical condition. It is only to help direct people to the appropriate health-care provider if a problem is suspected. Don't forget that many babies have diaper rashes, ear infections and diarrhea on occasion and it is certainly normal for infants and children to touch their genitals. But if you read this list and suspect your child may have a health problem related to yeast, it's important to seek treatment from a care provider familiar with this illness.

TESTING FOR ALLERGIES

One of the most precise tests for food allergies is a new test called *provocation/neutralization*. Provocation utilizes the method of dropping an allergy extract under the tongue or into the skin. Neutralization refers to the second step, which involves administering a weaker dilution of the same extract intended to neutralize or eliminate the reaction caused by the provocation.

Another test involves a blood test called the RAST (Radioallergosorbent test) that, if positive, demonstrates a person is allergic to the substance tested, such as food, pollen, dust or molds.

DEALING WITH FOOD REACTIONS

Should you suspect allergy but are not sure which of the variety of foods your baby is eating is the offender, try eliminating the foods most likely to cause allergy. An allergist with up-to-date training and experience with current methods of detecting allergies can be consulted to help discover specific food allergies. Ask the physician if she is familiar with the latest tests available to discover food allergies.

If your child has a mild reaction to a given food, try waiting a few weeks before offering it again. If the same symptoms appear, eliminate that food from baby's diet. If baby has a violent reaction the first time a food is eaten, do not offer the food again. The risk is far too high. In rare instances, death has occurred as a result of a severe food allergy. If swelling of the tongue or throat occurs, baby needs immediate medical attention.

As you can see, food allergies are complex and not any fun for anyone involved. The best treatment for food allergy is prevention. If solid foods are introduced slowly, at not too early an age, and baby is given only one new food a week, parents have a better chance of preventing food allergies. Dr. Lendon Smith, a leading authority on nutrition, recommends: "No solids should be introduced until well after six months of age. It seems boring, but it is safe as it may preclude the development of allergies."

The pages that follow include feeding information helpful for a child allergic to milk, eggs or wheat. There is a sample food diary on page 68 where you can record baby's reactions to new foods.

THE MILK-FREE DIET

Milk is one of the most common foods causing allergy. Waiting until after baby's first birthday to introduce milk seems to decrease the chance of an allergic response. It does not, however, guarantee none will occur. Look for symptoms of allergy (listed above) when milk is introduced and stop feeding your child milk if symptoms appear.

There are two types of adverse reactions to milk: (1) *lactose intolerance* and (2) *milk allergy*. Some people have a lactose intolerance, meaning their bodies have difficulty digesting milk. This is because they lack lactase, the enzyme responsible for the digestion of lactose (milk sugar). Symptoms of a milk intolerance are abdominal cramps, bloating, diarrhea and gas. Children (or adults) with a milk intolerance often can eat yogurt since the fermenting process involved has already broken down the milk sugar, making it easier to digest. Lactase can be purchased to add to whole milk (24 hours before using it) to make it more digestible for the intolerant person. Lactase-treated milk products are now available next to the regular milk at your grocery store.

A milk allergy is more severe than a milk intolerance. People with a milk allergy must avoid all milk and milk products. Yogurt or lactase-treated products would not benefit them since they are allergic to the milk itself.

Once it is known or suspected a child is allergic to milk, alternatives need to be found. The knowledge of which foods are necessary to avoid is very important.

Foods to Avoid on a Milk-Free Diet

- All milk beverages: milk, milkshakes, cocoa, chocolate milk, half-and-half, condensed milk, evaporated milk, skim milk, 1 percent milk, 2 percent milk, powdered milk, dried milk, milk solids, and curds and whey
- Butter, margarine (check labels: some margarine is milk-free)
- Cream, sour cream, whipping cream, buttermilk
- Cheeses (including cottage cheese)

- Yogurt
- Custards
- Breads made with milk or milk products, biscuits, muffins, pancakes, waffles, crackers
- Cookies, cakes, ice cream, puddings, doughnuts, pies and desserts made with milk or milk products
- Creamed soups, vegetables, sauces, gravies
- Canned or dehydrated soups made with milk or milk products
- Milk chocolate
- Mashed potatoes
- Salad dressings containing milk or milk products
- Casein, sodium caseinate and lactalbumin (proteins in milk).

Watch closely for these when reading labels.

Once you know or suspect your child is allergic to milk, consult immediately with a health-care provider who has knowledge and experience in dealing with milk allergies.

When avoiding milk in the diet, the following liquids can be substituted: soy milks, soy formulas, nondairy creamers (avoid brands containing sodium caseinate), coconut milk (avoid brands containing sodium caseinate) and nut milks.

EGG-FREE DIET

Eggs provide excellent nutrients, including protein, fat and iron, but are *not* an essential part of a diet. The egg yolk contains a high concentration of cholesterol (one large egg yolk contains approximately 250 to 275 milligrams of cholesterol). Watching out for foods containing eggs can be tricky, so label reading is a must.

Many childhood vaccines (such as polio, measles and influenza) are cultured on eggs, causing allergic symptoms to appear in people who are extremely sensitive to eggs. Consult your child's doctor if you even suspect egg allergy in your child. Some people who are allergic to eggs also are allergic to chicken.

Egg Substitutes

There seem to be few good substitutes for eggs, but a little bit of tofu (about two ounces) sometimes can work quite well in recipes. Some recipes that call for one or two eggs can be replaced with a tablespoon or two of water. Baked goods are a little trickier. A mashed banana can be substituted for an egg in a muffin recipe if you don't mind the banana taste. Experimentation and imagination will be helpful here.

The egg substitutes found in the supermarket are not always egg-free. These are made for people concerned with low-cholesterol diet, so read the labels. Most natural food store sell eggless egg substitutes.

Foods to Avoid on an Egg-Free Diet

- Beverages made with eggs: eggnog, malted shakes, root beer
- Noodles or pasta made with eggs
- Desserts made with eggs: ice cream, cookies, cakes, cream pies, meringue pies, custards, sherbets, candies
- Hollandaise sauce, tartar sauce
- Bread products made with eggs, breaded foods
- Pancakes, waffles, French toast
- Doughnuts
- Pretzels
- Dried or powdered eggs
- Egg white or yolks
- Egg white solids
- Egg albumen
- Mayonnaise, salad dressings containing eggs
- Meatloaf or meat dishes containing eggs
- Cake mixes or other prepared mixes containing egg products or egg ingredients
- Egg dishes (scrambled, baked, fried or boiled eggs, omelets, quiches, souffles)
- Poultry or fish dishes containing eggs
- Baking powders that contain egg white or albumen
- Coffee or wine if clarified with egg white or shell
- Soups, any soup containing egg products or ingredients

WHEAT-FREE DIET

Wheat is another food that frequently causes allergic reactions. Rice, barley and oats usually are the first cereals offered baby in order to avoid possible allergic reactions.

Foods to Avoid on a Wheat-Free Diet

- Flour: white, whole wheat, enriched, unbleached, graham
- Wheat bran or wheat germ
- Wheat gluten or wheat starch

- Malt, malted milk
- Farina
- Monosodium glutamate
- Breads, biscuits, muffins, rolls, crackers, pretzels
- Doughnuts
- Pancakes, waffles
- Bread crumbs
- Pasta
- Desserts made with flour (pies, cakes, cookies, candies)
- Coffee substitutes
- Ovaltine
- Most beers, gin and whiskey
- Gravy, sauces, tamari sauce
- Processed cheese (some contain wheat stabilizers)
- Some meat products (canned meats, hot dogs, sausage, meatloaf, lunch meats)

Good substitutions for 1 cup wheat flour:
1¼ cups rye flour
1⅓ cups oat flour
⅝ cup potato starch (potato flour)
⅞ cup rice flour
¾ cup barley flour
¾ cup cornmeal

Experimentation and perseverance will be necessary when substituting other flours for wheat flour, since some recipes work better than others when substituting different types of flours.

Baby's Food Diary

Food Introduced	Baby's Age	Today's Date	Liked	Disliked	Adverse Reaction	Time Food Was Given	Time of Reaction

Chapter Eight

BEGINNER RECIPES (SIX MONTHS)

The beginner recipes are for six-month-old babies who are starting to eat solid foods. Early feeding need not be elaborate and baby doesn't need a wide variety of choices. This section contains recipes for cereals and fruits. A slow introduction of each new food is recommended (see chapter six, "How to Feed Your Baby"). Several time-saving ideas are included in this section:

- making large batches of fruits to puree and freeze in ice cube trays
- grinding grains ahead of time and storing in jars for daily use
- using a pressure cooker
- microwave tips

INTRODUCING SOLIDS

Here are a few more ideas for those first days of introducing solid foods to your baby:

1. Choose a nonfussy time to begin feeding solid food. Between bottles or nursing is usually a good time.
2. Start with small spoonfuls of each new food. Feed gently and in a relaxed manner.
3. Never save foods that baby doesn't finish. The serving spoon mixes saliva into the remaining food, and this saliva breaks down the food, causing a loss in nutritional value and freshness.
4. Take time to enjoy baby's mealtimes. Household chores will always be there, but your infant baby won't stay little very long. (Honest!) Have fun!

MICROWAVE TIPS

Microwave ovens can be used for cooking large batches of vegetables and fruits. Cooking times vary with different models, foods and amounts of foods. Check the manufacturer's instruction book to help guide you.

Microwave Safety Hints

Always check the temperature of the food before giving it to baby. (Remember that microwaves are *not* recommended for heating baby bottles since the liquid is heated unevenly and can cause severe and unexpected burns). Always use microwavable dishes (I prefer glass) since other plastic containers (such as margarine tubs) may melt and send carcinogenic substances into baby's food.

INTRODUCE (BEGINNING AT SIX MONTHS):

Fruits
> banana
> avocado
> papaya
> pears
> apples
> plums
> apricots

Offer one new food a week, all foods in pureed form. One meal a day can be given for the first weeks of feeding solids. Gradually increase to two meals.

Grains
> rice
> barley
> oats
> millet

Sample Menu for Beginners
> Breakfast: Rice cereal
> Dinner: Apple puree
> Plus: Breast milk or formula at least 3 times a day

AVOCADO-ADO!

2-3 tablespoons ripe peeled avocado

Mash with fork or blend through a baby food grinder. You can add breast milk or formula for the first few feedings.

A few words about the avocado: If you have never eaten an avocado, please don't toss this recipe aside. Avocados are a great first food for baby. They are soft, bland and high in vitamin A. Don't assume your baby won't like avocados if you have never tasted them—like I almost did! (Although this is primarily a baby food cookbook, a great way for grownups to taste avocados is by putting little chunks in a salad, or eating them with a bit of lemon juice, or making them into guacamole.) When choosing an avocado, purchase one that is soft (not mushy) to the touch, or buy a firm avocado and let it sit out a few days until it gets soft.

BANANA-ANA!

½ ripe banana, peeled

Mash with fork or put through a baby food grinder. Add a bit of breast milk or formula to thin for initial feedings.

AVOCADO BANANA CREAM
(affectionately called "That Green Stuff")

½ banana
¼-½ small avocado

Blend thoroughly in a baby food grinder.

FRUIT PUREE

> *Large quantity of fruit (babies like apples, pears, peaches, plums, apricots) washed, peeled and chopped*

Add ¼ cup boiling water to each cup of fruit. Simmer until tender. Blend everything (including water) in blender. Freeze remainder in ice cube trays. Thaw 2 or 3 cubes when needed. Fruit can be served warm or at room temperature.

Pressure cooker method: Place washed, peeled fruit (remove seeds) on rack and add 1 cup water. Do not fill pressure cooker over two-thirds full. Cook according to the timetable below, allowing pressure regulator to rock slowly during cooking. Cool cooker under faucet of cool running water until pressure drops to normal or according to manufacturer's directions. Puree in blender or food processor and freeze in ice cube trays.

Fruit	Cooking Time
apples (whole)	7 minutes
apricots (whole)	2 minutes
peaches (whole)	5 minutes
pears (whole)	6-8 minutes
plums	2 minutes

DRIED FRUIT PUREE

> *1 cup dried fruit (apricots, papayas, peaches, pears, apples)*
> *Water to cover*

Place in covered container and soak overnight in refrigerator. Pour into the blender the next day and puree. Serve and refrigerate remainder no more than 3 days.

DRIED FRUIT PUREE
(Quick Method)

Put fruit and water in saucepan, cover and simmer until soft (10-20 minutes). Puree in blender. Great mixed with yogurt or cereal.

Pressure cooker method: Place dried fruit on rack and add water to cover. Do not fill pressure cooker over two-thirds full. Cook according to timetable below, allowing pressure regulator to rock slowly during cooking. Cool cooker under faucet of cool running water until pressure drops to normal. Puree in blender or food processor and freeze in ice cube trays.

Dried Fruit	Cooking Time
apples	6-8 minutes
apricots	6-8 minutes
figs	20-25 minutes
papaya	8-10 minutes
peaches	6-8 minutes
pears	6-8 minutes
prunes	6-8 minutes

Note: Cooking time varies depending on fruit size, so use the longer cooking time for the larger-size fruits.

RICE CEREAL

1 cup water, breast milk or formula
¼ cup rice powder (brown rice ground in blender*)

In saucepan, bring liquid to boil. Sprinkle in rice powder, stirring constantly. Simmer covered for 10 minutes. This is good with pureed fruit. Serve warm.

* To grind large amounts of rice, barley, millet or oatmeal, place ¾ cup of grain in the blender and whiz at high speed 20-30 seconds. Store in sterile glass jars. (Oatmeal can be ground in a food processor but the other grains do better in the blender.)

BARLEY CEREAL

1 cup breast milk, water or formula
¼ cup ground barley (ground in the blender)

Bring liquid to a boil. Add barley and simmer 10 minutes. Serve warm. (Add more liquid for thinner consistency.)

OATMEAL

> ¼ cup ground oats (don't use the instant kind—just grind regular
> oatmeal in blender or food processor)
> ¾ cup water

Bring water to boil. Add oats, cover, simmer 5 minutes. Serve warm
with added breast milk or formula, apple juice or pureed fruit.

MILLET CEREAL

> 1 cup breast milk, water or formula
> 3 tablespoons ground millet

Bring liquid to a boil. Add millet, stirring constantly for a minute. Simmer 10 minutes. Serve warm.

RICE, OAT OR BARLEY CEREAL
(Method 2)

Cook grains (without grinding them first) by normal method, omitting
salt (see page 85 for cooking time). After grains are cooked, blend in
the blender or food processor until smooth. This is an easy way to cook
cereal when other children or family members are eating the same foods
together.

COMBINATION CEREAL

> ¾ to 1 cup water
> 1 tablespoon ground oats
> 1 tablespoon ground rice
> 1 tablespoon ground barley

Bring water to a boil. Add grains and stir with wire whip. Cover and
simmer 10 minutes. Serve warm.

Chapter Nine

INTERMEDIATE RECIPES (SEVEN TO NINE MONTHS)

Intermediates (seven- to nine-month-olds) are getting the knack of being spoon-fed. Most of them are ready to venture into the world of vegetables and different cereal combinations. Introduced in this section are recipes for vegetables, cereal, yogurt, smoothies, tofu and various lunch ideas. Baby should now be eating two meals a day plus juice or a smoothie snack. Look for possible milk allergy after introducing yogurt and other milk and cheese products.

INTRODUCE: (SEVEN TO NINE MONTHS)

Mild vegetables
   carrots
   green beans
   peas
   zucchini
   squash

Yogurt

Egg yolk (cooked)

Beverages
   mild juices — apple, apricot,
   papaya
   smoothies

Tofu

Cheese

Continue introducing one new food per week. Begin combining fruits with cereals. Juice or smoothie can be given for an occasional snack. Bagel, biscuits or bread can be given to help with teething. Watch closely for choking or gagging. Gradually increase to three meals a day. Continue to puree most foods but begin to offer thicker, lumpier foods. Watch for food allergy.

Sample Menu for Intermediates
  Breakfast: Oatmeal plus apple juice
  Lunch: Tofu-banana whip or smoothie
  Dinner: Baby vegetable puree
  Plus: Breast milk or formula 2-3 times a day

BABY VEGETABLE PUREE

Large quantity of fresh vegetables (choose from carrots, green beans, peas, zucchini, etc.)

Add at least 2 inches of water in saucepan. Cover and cook until tender. Blend; serve warm. Freeze remainder in ice cube trays.

Pressure cooker method: Using a pressure cooker to cook vegetables saves most of the valuable vitamins and minerals that can escape during regular cooking. Clean and chop vegetables; add ½ to 1 cup water and cook according to pressure cooker directions. Don't forget to include the cooking water when you puree vegetables in the blender. This method allows you to prepare a large quantity at a time.

STEAMED VEGETABLES

2 cups chopped fresh vegetables
1½ cups water

In a saucepan, bring water to a boil under the steam basket. Place vegetables in basket and check water level to be sure water is not touching vegetables. Cover and steam until tender (usually about 10 minutes, if vegetables are cut small). Blend; serve. Freeze remainder.

HOMEMADE YOGURT

4 cups milk
¼ cup nonfat dry milk (optional but good to add when using low-fat or skim milk because it makes a thicker, creamier yogurt)
2 tablespoons unpasteurized plain yogurt or 1 package dried yogurt culture (purchase at natural foods store)

In a small bowl, add nonfat milk to 1 cup milk and stir until dissolved.

Pour into saucepan and add remaining 3 cups milk. Mix well. Heat over low heat until milk starts to bubble around the edges of the saucepan. Remove from heat and cool to 105°F to 115°F. (Milk should feel very warm if tested on the wrist.) Remove 1 cup warm milk and place in a small bowl. Stir in yogurt or yogurt culture until dissolved. Add to remaining milk and stir again. Pour into individual containers of a yogurt maker or into sterile glass jars. Cover. Incubate in yogurt maker for 6 to 10 hours or use one of the following methods:

1. Place jars of yogurt on a heating pad and wrap tightly with towels or a small blanket.
2. Place in electric oven on lowest possible temperature.
3. Place a hot-water bottle at the bottom of a large cooking pot. Place yogurt on top and cover tightly. Wrap pan in towels.
4. Place in metal cooking pan and place close to wood stove.
   (A constant temperature of 110°F is ideal during incubation period.)

Helpful Yogurt-Making Tips

- If using homemade yogurt, be sure it is used before it is more than five days old.
- Do not use yogurt that contains stabilizers — read labels closely.
- Be gentle with yogurt. Fold gently when adding yogurt to other ingredients.
- Do not add fruit to yogurt during cooking time. Dried fruits should be added right before yogurt is put in the refrigerator. Other fruits should be added at serving time.
- Yogurt tastes best if used within two weeks. After that time, yogurt is best used in cooking since it develops a sharper flavor.

FRUIT YOGURT*

3 tablespoons plain yogurt (not low-fat)
2 tablespoons pureed fruit (apples, peaches, bananas, apricots)

Mix together and serve. Most babies will love yogurt, even if their parents don't!

Note: The higher fat content in whole milk makes it easier to digest in infants than yogurt made with skim milk. If baby is overweight, the switch to lowfat yogurt can be made at age one.

* No berries until age two.

SMOOTHIES

½ cup fruit (peaches, papaya, bananas, apricots)
½ cup milk (breast milk or formula before age one)
¼ cup whole milk yogurt (plain)*
¼ teaspoon vanilla extract
1 teaspoon blackstrap molasses (or honey after age one)

Blend in blender. Serves baby plus one!

*Although yogurt is easily digested and usually well tolerated by infants, a child with an allergy to milk will have an allergic reaction to yogurt because it is a milk product. If any reaction occurs, stop all milk products and check with the pediatrician for suggestions on when to reintroduce milk into baby's diet.

SIMPLE BANANA SMOOTHIE

½ cup plain yogurt
½ banana
¼ teaspoon blackstrap molasses (or honey after age one)
Dash of vanilla

Combine all ingredients in a blender. Serve at once. One serving. (Double the recipe if you want enough for a thirsty toddler or thirsty grownup.)

OATMEAL PLUS

1¼ cups water
¼ cup oatmeal (rice or barley can also be used)
¼ cup chopped dates, raisins, peaches or apricots
1 teaspoon finely ground almonds (optional)

Bring water to a boil. Add remaining ingredients. Cover and simmer for 5 minutes. Puree in grinder or blender. Serve warm.

TOFU-BANANA WHIP
(Often called "toe-food" around our house)

½ banana
1 tablespoon tofu

Mash with fork and blend until smooth. Great on rice cakes or peanut butter bread.

Note: Tofu is made from soybeans in a way similar to the way cheese is made from milk. It looks like a cube of ricotta cheese, but it really has a very bland taste. It is full of protein, low in calories, and for these reasons it is a great "extender" food. Store tofu in the refrigerator and keep it covered with water. If the water is changed daily (or almost every day) tofu will last up to ten days. If it doesn't smell fresh, don't use it. Draining tofu on a paper towel helps remove excess water before combining it with other ingredients. Tofu is usually found in the produce department at your grocery store or in natural food stores. Check the date to ensure freshness.

BABY RICE PUDDING

½ cup brown rice
2 cups milk (formula, breast milk or water before age one)
1 egg yolk (or whole egg after age one)
¼ teaspoon vanilla extract
1 teaspoon blackstrap molasses

Rinse rice. Combine all ingredients in saucepan. Bring to a boil; then simmer 1 hour. (Check to see if more liquid needs to be added.) Let cool. Put through blender or baby food grinder. Good served warm or cold.

COTTAGE CHEESE LUNCH*

Combine 3 tablespoons of cottage cheese with one of the following:
3 tablespoons applesauce
3 tablespoons pureed fruit
2 thawed fruit puree cubes (apples, peaches, pears, apricots)
¼ small ripe avocado, mashed

Blend in baby food grinder and serve.

* Be on the lookout for milk allergy after introducing cottage cheese.

Chapter Ten

ADVANCED RECIPES (TEN TO TWELVE MONTHS)

Advanced" babies are getting more lovable by the minute. These ten-, eleven- and twelve-month-olds are sprouting a few teeth (some babies' first teeth arrive later so don't panic if you have a toothless babe now) and good, strong gums. These babies begin to see a lot of options available on their menu. Grains, beans, egg yolks and a wider variety of vegetables are available for them. Begin watching for wheat or egg allergies and be careful not to overfeed. Remember to let baby use teeth and gums to chew or mix the food.

INTRODUCE: (TEN TO TWELVE MONTHS)

Legumes
  cooked dried beans and peas
  thinned peanut butter and nut
    butters
  ground sprouts

Grains
  bulgur
  wheat

Meals can begin to be in less pureed form but avoid large chunks of food. Finger foods can be offered. Continue to watch for reactions or allergies to any new (or old) food. Advanced babies can have three meals a day plus occasional juice and healthy snacks.

Vegetables
stronger vegetables — broccoli, cabbage, cauliflower

Cheese
small cheese cubes
shredded melted cheese

Sample Menu for Advanced Babies
Breakfast: Whole Wheat Pancakes with fruit puree, apple or papaya juice
Lunch: Bunny Yogurt or Carrot-Zucchini Shred
Dinner: Rice 'n Beans and mashed carrot or soft carrot pieces or Garden Casserole and whole wheat bread or crackers
Plus: Breast milk or formula three times a day

BULGUR & VEGETABLES

¾ cup boiling water
⅓ cup bulgur
2 tablespoons grated zucchini
2 tablespoons grated carrot
1 tablespoon shredded cheese (optional)

Bring water to a boil in a saucepan. Sprinkle bulgur, zucchini and carrot into water and stir briefly. Cover and let stand for 5 minutes. Put through baby food grinder. Sprinkle with cheese and stir. Serve warm.

LENTILS & RICE

¼ cup cooked lentils
¾ cup cooked brown rice

Blend together and puree with a little cooking water from the lentils. Serve warm. This makes 2 servings.

RICE 'N BEANS

> 3 tablespoons cooked brown rice
> 1 tablespoon cooked beans (pinto, black or other beans)
> 2 tablespoons cooking water from beans
> 1 tablespoon shredded cheese

Mix all ingredients. Heat in a saucepan until cheese melts. Blend through grinder or serve as is, if baby is receptive to lumpy food. This is an excellent main meal protein dish.

BROCCOLI & RICE

> ¼ cup chopped, cooked broccoli
> ½ cup cooked brown rice or bulgur
> ¼ cup cooked barley
> ¼ cup cooking water from broccoli
> 2 tablespoons grated cheese

Combine first four ingredients and heat in a saucepan (no longer than 2-3 minutes, since broccoli and grains are already cooked). Put through a baby food grinder and top with cheese or serve as is if your baby can chew lumpy food. Enough for 2 servings (one for dinner and one re-heated the next day for lunch).

CARROT 'N BEAN SOUP

> 1 carrot, chopped
> 1 cup green beans, chopped
> 2 cups water

Place ingredients in a saucepan. Cover. Simmer until tender (about 30 minutes, depending on size of cut vegetables). Blend carrots, beans and cooking water together in blender. Serve warm. For a large batch, just increase all ingredients proportionately. Freeze in ice cube trays.

Pressure cooker method: Double the recipe above but decrease the water to 3 cups. Cook 8 minutes after pressure regulator begins to rock.

Bean Preparation

Use 1 Cup of	Soaking Required	Water	Cooking Time	Approx. Yield
Baby limas use in casseroles, side dishes	Yes	2 cups	1½ hrs.	1¾ cups
Black-eyed peas use in main dishes, southern cookery	Yes	3 cups	1 hr.	2 cups
Black (turtle) beans use in soups, Mexican dishes	Yes	4 cups	1½ hrs.	2 cups
Garbanzos (chick peas) use in soups, salads, dips	Yes	4 cups	2½-3 hrs.	2 cups
Great Northern beans use in baked beans, soups, main dishes	Yes	3½ cups	2 hrs.	2 cups
Kidney beans use in chili, Mexican dishes	Yes	3 cups	1½-2 hrs.	2 cups
Lentils use in soups, casseroles	No	3 cups	1 hr.	2¼ cups
Lima beans use in side dishes, casseroles	Yes	2 cups	1½-2 hrs.	1¼ cups
Navy beans (white beans) use in main dishes	Yes	3 cups	2½-3 hrs	2 cups

Use 1 Cup of	Soaking Required	Water	Cooking Time	Approx. Yield
Pea beans use in baked beans	Yes	3 cups	2 hrs.	2 cups
Pinto beans use in refried beans, chili, main dishes, Mexican dishes	Yes	3 cups	2 hrs.	2 cups
Soybeans use in soups, main dishes, casseroles	Yes	4 cups	3 hrs.	2 cups
Split peas use in soups, main dishes	No	3 cups	1 hr.	2¼ cups

How to Cook Beans

Rinse beans well under cold running water. Discard any cracked beans and small rocks while rinsing. Soak beans overnight. (Soybeans must be soaked in the refrigerator, but all other beans can remain at room temperature.) Place beans and water in a saucepan (use soaking water and add more water if necessary). Cover loosely and simmer for approximate amount of time specified above. Do not add salt or oil during cooking. A clove of garlic or small onion may be added if desired. Test beans for tenderness and adjust cooking time accordingly since the exact time varies.

Quick soak method: Forget to soak the beans the night before? Bring water and beans to a boil. Simmer 2-3 minutes, then cover and let soak for 2 hours. Cook beans according to above directions.

How to Cook Grains

Bring water to boil in a saucepan. Slowly sprinkle grain into boiling water. Cover and simmer over low heat for the amount of time specified in above chart. Do not add salt during cooking time.

Cooking Grains

Use 1 Cup of	Water	Cooking Time	Approx. Yield
Barley	3 cups	1 hr., 15 min.	3½ cups
Brown rice	2 cups	1 hr.	3 cups
Buckwheat groats (Kasha)	2 cups	15 min.	2½ cups
Bulgur wheat	2 cups	15-20 min.	2½ cups
Cracked wheat	2 cups	25 min.	3 cups
Cornmeal	4 cups	25 min.	3 cups
Millet	3 cups	45 min.	3½ cups
Oatmeal	2 cups	15 min.	2 cups
Whole wheat berries	3 cups	1 hr.	2¼ cups
Wild rice	3 cups	1 hr.	4 cups
Basmati rice	1 cup	20 minutes	2½ cups

RICE-SQUASH

1 tablespoon brown rice
1 tablespoon squash (acorn, green, yellow)

Cook rice until almost tender, about 40 minutes. Add squash pieces and complete cooking. Blend in blender or grinder. (This is good to have when rice is included in the family menu.)

COLORFUL BARLEY

1 cup water
1 tablespoon uncooked barley, ground fine
1 tablespoon peas
½ carrot, grated

Bring water to a boil. Sprinkle barley powder in with wire whip. Add peas and grated carrot. Simmer 15 minutes or until vegetables are tender. Serve warm.

GARDEN CASSEROLE

Broccoli
Cauliflower
Carrots
Potatoes
Cheese

Chop vegetables and steam until tender. Top with a bit of baby's favorite cheese and serve warm.

LENTIL CHEESEBURGERS

½ cup lentils
1 egg yolk
1 tablespoon whole wheat bread crumbs or wheat germ
Dash of thyme (optional)
Monterey Jack or Swiss cheese slices (optional)

Cook lentils until soft so they mash easily with a fork, about 1 hour. Drain any excess water and save for soup stock. When lentils are cool, add egg yolk, bread crumbs and thyme. Shape into patties. Bake 15 minutes at 350°F. Top with cheese slices and return to oven until cheese melts. Serve warm. (Be sure cheese has cooled to avoid a bad burn.)

WHOLE WHEAT PANCAKES

⅓ to ½ cup whole wheat flour
1 teaspoon baking powder
1½ teaspoons honey
½ cup milk
1 egg yolk or 1 tablespoon tofu
1½ teaspoons vegetable oil

Combine dry ingredients. Combine liquid ingredients. Stir into dry ingredients only until moistened. Cook in lightly oiled skillet. Enough for

2 servings. Refrigerate leftover pancakes for next day. Reheat briefly in dry skillet—just till warm. Serve with yogurt and fruit.

Note: Pancakes are great for any meal, but lunchtime pancakes are usually a favorite with babies and toddlers. Babies enjoy picking up bite-size pieces and feeding themselves.

ZUCCHINI PANCAKES

1 zucchini, grated
1 egg yolk (whole egg after age one)
2 tablespoons mashed tofu (optional—this can replace the egg)
½ cup whole wheat flour
⅓ cup milk
¼ teaspoon baking powder

Mix all ingredients just until moistened. Cook in oiled skillet until lightly browned, just like regular pancakes. This is a great finger-food favorite! Save leftovers and reheat the next day. These also freeze well.

POTATO PANCAKES

2 potatoes, shredded fine or processed in food processor
1 egg yolk (whole egg after age one) or 1 tablespoon tofu
2 tablespoons flour

Combine all ingredients in mixing bowl. Pour batter by large spoonfuls onto oiled skillet. Flip when edges turn lightly brown. Serve at room temperature. This is another good finger food!

COTTAGE CHEESE PANCAKES

½ cup cottage cheese
1 egg yolk
½ cup whole wheat flour
⅓ cup milk
¼ teaspoon baking powder

Mix all ingredients. Cook in lightly oiled skillet until lightly browned on both sides. Good topped with applesauce.

APPLE DELIGHT

½ *apple, pared*
½ *banana*
½ *carrot*
¼ *cup apple juice*

Whiz in blender until smooth. This can be spoon fed to baby or served in a cup with larger holes in the lid. Apple Delight is a wonderful lunch served with a muffin or toast!

VEGETABLE LUNCH

2 *tablespoons zucchini, finely grated*
1 *tablespoon alfalfa sprouts (optional)*
2 *tablespoons carrot, finely grated*

Whiz in blender. Add yogurt for a different treat.
A word about sprouts: Sprouts have sprouted up (oh, no) in the produce section of most grocery stores. These are full of protein and a great addition to salads as well as other foods. They are easy to grow in your own kitchen.

Equipment Needed for Sprouting

Wide-mouth quart jar, sterile
2 layers of cheesecloth or nylon net or a washcloth
Rubber band or ring of a Mason jar

How to Sprout

1. Rinse seeds or beans and sort out any that are cracked, discolored or damaged. Soak 1 tablespoon seeds or ⅓ cup beans overnight in a clean jar filled with one quart of warm water.
2. In the morning, secure cheesecloth over the jar opening with a rubber band. Pour out rinse water through the cheesecloth and rinse seeds thoroughly with warm water. (Fill jar with water and pour out; repeat several times.)
3. Turn jar upside down to let the water drain. Store sprouts on the kitchen counter or in a cupboard (sprouts will grow in dark or light area; however, mung bean sprouts grow best in the dark).

Keep jar out of direct sunlight. Be sure to drain well so seeds do not get moldy.

4. Gently rinse sprouts 2 or 3 times a day. Drain well.
5. When seeds are ready (check Sprout Growing chart for time) rinse in cold water. Drain well and store in refrigerator up to one week. The sooner the sprouts are used, the higher the nutritional value.
6. Bring alfalfa and other leafy sprouts out of the darkness the last day into indirect sunlight. The light provides a pretty green leaf and added chlorophyll.
7. Eat and enjoy the sprouts! They can be used in salads, sandwiches, breads and vegetable dishes. Children can easily grow sprouts with a little help from a grownup. Everyone enjoys watching them grow, and they taste so good!

Sprout Growing

Seeds*	Sprouting Time	Especially Good in:
Alfalfa	4 to 5 days	Salads, sandwiches, vegetable dishes
Garbanzo beans	3 days	Salads, sandwiches, soups, vegetable dishes
Lentils	3 to 4 days	Salads, soups, vegetable dishes
Mung beans	3 to 4 days	Salads, soups, Chinese dishes
Radish	3 to 4 days	Salads, sandwiches
Sunflower	2 days	Salads, sandwiches, breads, vegetable dishes
Soybeans**	3 days	Soups, cooked vegetable dishes
Wheat berries	2 days	Breads, vegetable dishes

*Be sure to purchase untreated seeds meant for eating and cooking, not planting. Seeds for planting are often chemically treated and should not be sprouted.

**Soybean sprouts must not be eaten raw since they contain a protein-inhibiting enzyme. Steam soybean sprouts 5 minutes before eating.

CARROT SALAD

7-8 presoaked raisins
2 tablespoons finely grated carrot
2 tablespoons finely grated apple
1 tablespoon yogurt

Soak raisins in ½ cup water at breakfast so they'll be soft by lunchtime. Be sure to blend raisins thoroughly in a blender or food grinder at this age. Wait until age two to introduce whole raisins since they can cause choking. Blend all ingredients through a baby food grinder and serve.

BUNNY YOGURT

3 tablespoons carrot, finely grated
3 tablespoons yogurt

Blend and serve.

BUNNY YOGURT II

2 tablespoons carrot, grated
2 tablespoons raw broccoli, grated
2-3 tablespoons plain yogurt

Blend through a baby food grinder and serve. This makes a nice lunch served with whole wheat toast and milk or juice.

CARROT-ZUCCHINI SHRED

½ carrot, grated
½ zucchini, grated

Steam carrot and zucchini in steamer 10 minutes or until soft. Blend through grinder with 2 tablespoons cooking water or serve as is to older baby. This can also be served raw after whizzing through processor or blender.

BAKED SWEET POTATOES

Bake sweet potato in 350°F oven for 1 hour. Scoop out potato and mash with a fork. Serve warm. Use a bit of apple juice or other liquid to cool potato.

POTATOES DELUXE

½ baked potato, shredded
¼ cup cottage cheese
1-2 tablespoons formula or breast milk

Combine potato and cottage cheese. Add liquid to thin mixture so it's suitable for baby. Serve. This is a great way to use leftover baked potatoes.

APPLED SWEET POTATOES

1 medium sweet potato, baked
½ cup apple, pureed, or ½ cup applesauce
¼ cup breast milk, formula or apple juice

Skin and mash baked sweet potato. Add applesauce and liquid. Mix gently. Place in lightly buttered baking dish. Cover. Bake 30 minutes at 350°F. Makes 2-3 servings. Leftovers can be reheated the next day.

This recipe takes a little more time than usual, but it's a real favorite! This is a good recipe to plan when your family menu includes sweet potatoes.

BAKED ACORN SQUASH

1 acorn squash
1 tablespoon honey

Slice acorn squash in half. Scoop out seeds. Add honey to the center of each half. Bake on foil-lined pan at 350°F for 45 minutes or until tender. Greatly appreciated by adults, too!

PEANUT BUTTER DELIGHT

½ banana, mashed
2 tablespoons peanut butter
2 tablespoons tofu

Blend in baby food grinder and serve. Thin with breast milk or formula, if necessary. This is good on rice cakes or whole wheat toast, too.

ELIZABETH'S PEANUT BUTTER PUDDING

2 tablespoons peanut butter
2 tablespoons applesauce or pureed apple
½ banana

Blend through a baby food grinder or mash with fork. Serve at room temperature.

BABY'S FIRST BIRTHDAY CAKE

4 tablespoons brown sugar
2 cups whole wheat flour (or 1 cup unbleached and 1 cup whole wheat)
½ teaspoon salt
2 teaspoons cinnamon
2 teaspoons baking soda
3 eggs
1½ cups vegetable oil
1 cup honey
2 cups carrots, grated

Grease a 9″ × 13″ pan. Mix all dry ingredients and sift. Beat eggs, oil and honey. Add to dry ingredients and mix. Add carrots. Bake 30 minutes at 350°F. Top with cream cheese icing.

CREAM CHEESE ICING

2 8-ounce packages cream cheese or Neufchatel cheese
¼ cup cooked honey
1 teaspoon vanilla
1 tablespoon butter (optional)

Have cream cheese at room temperature. Blend all ingredients.

Note: Cream cheese is high in saturated fat and not high on the list of cheeses that offer quality nutrients. It should be used sparingly or can be replaced with kefir cheese, yogurt cheese, Neufchatel cheese, tofu or low-fat cottage cheese whipped in the blender.

GINGERBREAD SHORTCAKE

½ cup butter
1 cup molasses
1 cup sour cream or yogurt
2⅓ cups flour
Dash salt
¾ teaspoon baking soda
1 teaspoon cinnamon
1 teaspoon ground ginger
¼ teaspoon ground cloves
2 bananas, sliced
Whipping cream

Combine butter and molasses in a small saucepan and bring to a boil. Add sour cream or yogurt. Sift all dry ingredients and add to molasses mixture and stir. Pour into square baking pan and bake at 350°F for 40 minutes. At serving time, remove from pan and cut into squares. Split squares into two layers and place sliced bananas between the layers. Top with whipped cream. This is especially good served warm on a special occasion.

Chapter Eleven

TODDLE FOOD RECIPES (ONE TO THREE YEARS)

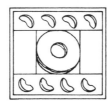

As baby begins to toddle about (at around age one), then run about (here come the terrific twos and threes!), she needs especially nutritious foods available when she stops for a moment to grab a bite to eat. And often "a bite to eat" is all she'll settle for. She is too busy exploring her fascinating world. It seems at times as if two-year-olds live on air. Other times they'll attempt to clean out your refrigerator—with or without your help!

Nutritious finger foods are essential for toddlers. Here are a few foods they can grab on the run: cheese cubes, rice cakes, puffed cereals, crackers, fruit pieces, muffins, bagels, toast and fresh vegetables. When toddlers feel like a real "meal" they can be given many good foods from the grownups' menu. Various beverages and frozen "popsicles" can provide essential vitamins and minerals between "meals."

Along with a variety of recipes especially enjoyed by toddlers, I've included two recipes to help out mom or dad on a cold or rainy day. Laura's Play Dough and Kid's Stuff are two nonedible recipes to help make the day more enjoyable for all. Have fun during this wonderful, growing and toddling time!

INTRODUCE (ONE TO THREE YEARS):
Nutritious finger foods, new vegetables, fruits or grains

Sample Menu for Toddlers
Breakfast: Granola or Familia with milk or yogurt, orange juice
Snack: fruit pieces

Three meals a day plus a snack or two can be given. Foods are lumpier and rarely need to be blended in the baby food grinder. Be sure all snacks are healthy ones since toddlers do not always stop to eat a complete meal. Continue to watch closely for signs of allergy.

Lunch: Cottage Cheese Delight, Oatmeal Muffin and Banana Smoothie

Snack: Molly's Juice Bar or vegetable pieces

Dinner: Whole Wheat Pizza and salad or Falafel Burgers in pita bread, green beans

Plus: 2-3 servings of milk or yogurt

SUNNY SMOOTHIE

¼ cup yogurt or milk
¼ cup orange juice
½ banana
¼ teaspoon blackstrap molasses or 1 teaspoon honey
Dash of vanilla

Blend well in blender. Serve at once. A great dessert treat!

CAROB MILK

1 cup milk
1 tablespoon melted carob chips or 1 tablespoon carob powder
2 teaspoons honey

Blend in blender and drink. Serves 1.

CAROB DELIGHT

1 cup milk
2 teaspoons carob powder
2 teaspoons honey
1 teaspoon noninstant dry milk
¼ teaspoon lecithin granules (optional)

Blend all ingredients in the blender. Drink! Serves 1.

BROWN MONKEY SHAKE

> 1 cup milk
> 1 banana
> 2 teaspoons carob powder
> 1 teaspoon honey
> 1 teaspoon noninstant dry milk

Blend in blender. Serves 1.

BRONWYN'S SMOOSHIE

> 1 cup of crushed ice
> 1 banana
> 4 strawberries

Pour ice into blender and add banana and strawberries. Blend all ingredients in the blender until "smooshed." Serves 1 thirsty toddler. (I've heard this drink is also a favorite with teens!)

CRANBERRY PUNCH

> 48 ounces cranberry juice
> 1 46-ounce can unsweetened pineapple juice
> 1½ quarts (48 ounces) orange juice
> Juice from one lemon

Mix all juices together. Chill and serve over ice. This recipe makes enough to have for a few days and is a wonderful thirst-quenching drink. (It's fun to make punch ice cubes from this recipe too. Add the colorful cubes to the punch or to a glass of orange juice.)

GRANOLA

4 cups old-fashioned oats
1 cup sesame seeds
1 cup sunflower seeds
1 cup wheat germ (raw)
1 cup unsweetened coconut
½ cup noninstant dry milk
½ cup honey
½ cup safflower oil
1 teaspoon vanilla
½ cup almonds, chopped
½ cup raisins

Toss dry ingredients (except raisins and almonds) in a large bowl. Mix honey, oil and vanilla together and pour over oatmeal mixture. Stir. Pour onto baking sheet and bake in 300°F oven for 30 minutes, stirring several times. Add almonds and raisins during the last 5 minutes. Remove from oven and cool completely before storing in a large glass jar with a tight-fitting lid.

CORNMEAL CEREAL

1 cup water
¼ cup yellow cornmeal

Using a double boiler, bring water to a boil. Slowly sprinkle cornmeal into water, stirring constantly with a wire whip or wooden spoon. Simmer 15 minutes. Let stand 15 minutes. Add a dash of honey and thin with milk. Serves 1 toddler.

BEAR MUSH DELUXE

Cook one serving of Bear Mush (Arrowhead Mills packaged cereal). Add 1 tablespoon of honey and ¼ cup of chopped fruit (peaches, apricots, pears, apples) and you have a delicious warm cereal on a cold winter morning!

FRENCH TOAST

1 egg
2 tablespoons milk
2 slices whole wheat bread

Beat egg and milk together in a pie pan. Dip bread in egg mixture and place in oiled skillet. Cook until lightly browned on each side. Good served with honey butter and cinnamon, or your favorite fruit preserves.

HONEY BUTTER

½ cup butter
½ cup honey

Let butter soften at room temperature. Stir in honey with a fork. This is a great topping for waffles, pancakes or French toast. Refrigerate after use.

MEREDITH'S OMELET

1 egg
1 tablespoon milk
½ teaspoon butter
2 tablespoons grated cheese

Combine egg and milk and beat with a fork. Melt butter over low heat in a 7-inch skillet. Pour egg mixture into skillet and tilt skillet often so egg mixture becomes firm. Lift batter in some places with a fork so egg mixture touches hot skillet. When egg is cooked, add cheese and fold omelet in half. Keep in the skillet for 15 or more seconds and serve warm. Be careful that cheese has cooled enough for baby to eat safely. Green pepper, zucchini or shredded cooked potato can also be added for variation.

Note: Be sure egg mixture is entirely cooked. Also, be on the lookout for allergic reactions to eggs.

PITA-PINTO SANDWICH

½ cup cooked pinto beans, mashed (garbanzos or soybeans can also
be used)
Pita bread
Tomato slices
Avocado slices
Shredded cheese (optional)

Spread the beans into the pita bread, add tomato, avocado and cheese.
Serve as is or put under broiler for 5 minutes (be sure cheese is cooled
to avoid burns).

PEANUT BUTTER DELUXE SANDWICH

Peanut butter
Applesauce
Raisins (presoaked for toddlers under age two)
Crushed sunflower seeds

Mix all ingredients together and spread on whole wheat bread.

LUNCHEON BAGELS

Pizza bagel:
Spread bagel with *pizza sauce*
Top with *shredded mozzarella or provolone cheese*
Broil till cheese melts

Sprouts bagel:
Spread a lightly buttered, toasted bagel with:
Sliced tomato
Alfalfa sprouts
Provolone cheese
Broil till cheese melts

Cream cheese bagel:
Spread a lightly buttered, toasted bagel with:
Cream cheese
Ground walnuts (optional)

FLYNN'S FAVORITE BAGEL

Top bagel with Monterey Jack cheese slices (and nothing else) and place in toaster oven till cheese melts. (Check to be sure cheese is cooled enough to eat.) Serve with orange slices.

CHEESE MUFFIN

½ whole wheat muffin, toasted and lightly buttered
1 slice cheese (Muenster, Swiss, provolone or Colby)
1 slice tomato
1 tablespoon alfalfa sprouts

Layer toasted muffin half with tomato, sprouts and then the cheese. Broil 2 minutes or until cheese melts. Be sure to serve after the cheese has cooled.

CHEESE TORTILLAS

1 corn tortilla, buttered
Ricotta cheese or tofu
Grated Monterey Jack cheese
Sliced tomato

Place lightly buttered corn tortilla under the broiler for 2 minutes. Remove. Spread tortilla with ricotta or tofu, then tomato slices and top with the cheese. Broil until cheese melts. Cool to room temperature.

COTTAGE CHEESE DELIGHT

¼ cup cottage cheese
¼ cup pureed fruit (apples, pears, apricots, etc.)
2 tablespoons orange juice

Blend together and serve. This is a real favorite!

APPLESAUCE 'N RAISINS

½ cup applesauce
8 presoaked raisins

Blend in baby food grinder and serve.

CHICKIE DIP

Garbanzo (Chick Pea) Dip
½ cup water
1 cup cooked garbanzos (chick peas), mashed
⅓ cup safflower oil
3 tablespoons sesame seeds
½ teaspoon sea salt
1 clove garlic, crushed
3 tablespoons lemon juice

Blend in blender or food processor. Use as a dip with veggies or crackers or as a sandwich spread.

TODDLE SALAD

1 apple
8 presoaked raisins
2 tablespoons shredded carrot
3 tablespoons yogurt
1 teaspoon honey

Cut apple into bite-size pieces. Mix with raisins that have soaked overnight. Add carrot. Mix yogurt and honey, pour over salad. Serves 1.

LENTIL STEW

1 tablespoon celery, chopped
½ potato, cubed
½ carrot, grated
1 tablespoon oil
¼ cup washed lentils
1¼ cups water or vegetable broth
1 tomato, chopped, or ½ cup tomato juice

Saute celery, potato and carrot in oil. Add lentils, water and tomato. Bring to a boil. Cover and simmer 1 hour. Check to make sure liquid hasn't boiled out. Add more water if needed.

WHOLE WHEAT BISCUITS

2 cups whole wheat flour
2 tablespoons bran
1 tablespoon baking powder
¼ cup noninstant dry milk
½ teaspoon salt
⅓ cup safflower oil
¾ cup milk

Gently combine dry ingredients with wet ingredients. Knead 1 minute. Roll on floured cloth until ½-inch thick. Cut with biscuit cutter (star shapes or heart shapes are fun) and place on baking sheet. Bake at 450°F for 10 minutes. Makes 1 dozen.

CORN MUFFINS

1 cup cornmeal
¼ cup whole wheat flour
3 tablespoons soy flour (can be replaced with whole wheat flour, but
    the soy flour adds extra protein)
2 teaspoons baking powder
1 teaspoon salt
1 egg
1 cup milk
3 tablespoons noninstant dry milk
3 tablespoons honey
3 tablespoons oil

Combine dry ingredients. Mix all liquid ingredients. Add liquid mixture to dry ingredients and beat well. Bake in muffin cups or well-greased muffin tin at 375°F for 20 minutes.

PEANUT BUTTER BREAD

2½ cups whole wheat flour
1 tablespoon baking powder
1 teaspoon salt
1¼ cups milk
¼ cup honey
2 tablespoons oil
¾ cup peanut butter

Mix dry ingredients together. Set aside. Heat milk until warm. Add honey, oil and peanut butter to milk and stir well. Add liquid mixture to dry ingredients and blend well. Pour into well-greased bread pan and bake at 350°F for 40-50 minutes. This is delicious served with mashed banana.

RAISIN AND BRAN MUFFINS

3 cups bran
1 cup boiling water
2 eggs
1 cup honey
½ cup safflower oil
2 cups buttermilk
2¼ cups whole wheat flour
2 teaspoons baking soda
½ teaspoon sea salt
½ cup raisins

Mix bran and boiling water in a large bowl and set aside. In another bowl, mix the eggs, honey, oil and buttermilk. Add to the bran mixture. Sift together flour, baking soda and salt and stir into bran mixture. Add raisins. Bake at 375°F in muffin tins (oiled or papered) for 15 minutes. Serve with butter or honey. Makes 2 dozen.

OATMEAL MUFFINS

2 cups oats
1½ cups buttermilk
1 cup whole wheat flour
1 teaspoon baking soda
½ teaspoon salt
2 eggs, beaten
3 tablespoons honey

Mix oats with buttermilk. Set aside. Sift dry ingredients together and add to oat mixture. Stir in eggs and honey. Let mixture stand 20 minutes before baking. Bake at 375°F for 15-20 minutes in oiled or papered muffin tin. Makes 1 dozen.

MICHAEL'S CORN TORTILLAS

1½ cups water
3 tablespoons butter
1 cup cornmeal
1 teaspoon salt
1 cup whole wheat flour

In a saucepan, bring water to a boil. Add butter. Stir in cornmeal and cook over low heat for 5 minutes. Cool. Add salt to the flour and add to cornmeal mixture. (Add more water or flour if necessary.) Divide dough into 10-12 pieces. Roll out on floured bowl into flat circles. Cook on a hot griddle or skillet 1½ to 2 minutes each side. Watch closely so they do not burn. Stack on a large plate and keep covered with a cloth. Delicious with your favorite beans or cheese.

FROZEN BANANAS

Banana
Orange juice

Insert a popsicle stick in the banana (or in half a large banana). Dip in orange juice. Wrap in plastic wrap and freeze.

MOLLY'S JUICE BARS

Pour juice (apple, orange, grape, apricot, papaya) into molds or cups with popsicle sticks. These are good for teething babies, but are sometimes difficult for them to hold alone. (You'll often find teething babies gnawing on the handles.)

YOGURT POPSICLES

2 cups plain yogurt
1 6-ounce can concentrated, unsweetened fruit juice (orange, apricot, grape, apple)
1 teaspoon vanilla

Mix well and freeze in popsicle molds or small paper cups with popsicle sticks. These popsicles are also great for teething babies.

BANANA SPLITZ POPS

1 banana
1 cup plain yogurt
½ cup orange juice
Dash of vanilla or honey

Blend in blender and pour into popsicle molds. Freeze.

BANANA CRUNCHSICLES

1 banana
2 tablespoons melted carob chips
½ teaspoon safflower oil
1 teaspoon honey
Granola

Insert a popsicle stick in one end of the banana. Mix carob chips, oil and honey together and melt over double boiler. (An egg poacher is perfect.) Roll banana in melted carob mixture, then roll in granola. Freeze several hours.

PARTY CUBES

16 pineapple chunks
1 cup orange juice
1 cup cranberry juice
16 popsicle sticks

Place a small chunk of pineapple in each section of an ice cube tray. Mix juices together and pour over the pineapple. Insert a popsicle stick in each pineapple chunk. Freeze.

Serve one party cube to each child on a warm day. Closely supervise so there are no children running with popsicle sticks in their mouths and watch for possible allergic reactions to the pineapple.

SPECIAL DAY SUNDAE

1 scoop frozen yogurt
1 banana, sliced
½ cup fresh strawberries, sliced
1 tablespoon carob chips
Whipped cream

Scoop yogurt into a dish. Cover with banana slices, strawberries and carob chips. Top with a little fresh whipped cream.

PEANUT BUTTER 'N OATMEAL COOKIES

½ cup peanut butter
⅓ to ½ cup honey
1¼ cups old-fashioned oats
2 tablespoons dry milk
¼ teaspoon salt
¼ cup sunflower seeds (optional)

Mix peanut butter with honey. Add dry ingredients and mix. Drop by rounded teaspoonfuls on greased baking sheet. Bake 10 minutes at 350°F. Makes 2½ to 3 dozen.

OATMEAL COOKIES

1¾ cups flour
1 teaspoon sea salt
2 teaspoons baking powder
½ teaspoon cinnamon
⅓ cup safflower oil or softened butter
⅓ cup honey
⅓ cup molasses
2 eggs, beaten
2 cups old-fashioned oats
¾ cup raisins (optional; not for under age two)

Sift together flour, salt, baking powder and cinnamon. Combine oil, honey, molasses and eggs in another large bowl. Add dry ingredients and mix well. Add oats and mix again. Gently stir in raisins. Drop by rounded teaspoonfuls on greased cookie sheet. Bake at 350°F for 10-12 minutes. Makes 4 dozen.

LAURA'S PLAYDOUGH

(This is *not* to eat—but great for a rainy day project or a homemade birthday gift that children love.)

> 1 cup white flour
> ½ cup salt
> 2 tablespoons cream of tartar
> 1 tablespoon oil
> 1 cup water
> Few drops food coloring

Mix flour, salt, cream of tartar and oil in a saucepan. Add water and mix well. Cook over medium heat, stirring constantly, for 3 minutes. Dough will become difficult to stir and form a "clump" of dough. Cool slightly and knead for 5 minutes. Add food coloring during kneading process. This keeps a long time if stored in a tightly covered plastic container.

KID'S STUFF

(This recipe is *not* to eat—but another rainy-day activity for toddlers and caregivers to enjoy. Holiday ornaments can be crafted or any old shape can be cut with cookie cutters.)

> 3 cups flour
> 1½ cups cornstarch
> 1 tablespoon dry mustard or instant coffee
> 1 cup water

Combine dry ingredients in a large bowl. Pour in water, stirring constantly. Roll out on floured cloth or board and use cookie cutter for desired shapes, or shape and mold into shapes without cutting dough. Air-dry molded objects or bake 1 hour at 350°F. For a darker finish, brush first with milk and egg. Varnish when dry.

Chapter Twelve

WHOLE FAMILY RECIPES

This chapter contains recipes for the entire family ages 3 to 103! Baby can follow a natural, nutritious progression eating foods from the previous chapters then enjoying wholesome whole-family recipes from this chapter. Many of these recipes can also be shared with a toddling two, but check ingredients closely to be sure the recipe does not contain any foods that could cause problems (see chart on page 58).

BAKED APPLE PANCAKE

1 tablespoon oil
3 cups apples; sliced, peeled and cored
½ teaspoon cinnamon
½ teaspoon allspice
Juice from ½ lemon
½ cup whole wheat flour
¾ teaspoon baking powder
¼ cup honey
¼ cup yogurt or crumbled tofu
2 eggs

Preheat oven to 400°F. Heat oil into a large saucepan or skillet. Dump in the apples, cinnamon, allspice and lemon juice. Mix gently. Cover pan. Turn heat to medium and bring to a boil. When boiling, turn heat to low and simmer, covered, for 10 minutes. Remove from heat. Combine the flour and baking powder in a small mixing bowl. Pour in the honey, yogurt or tofu and eggs. Mix with a fork just until smooth, about 30 seconds. Grease a 9-inch pie pan. Put about one-third of the batter in the bottom of the pie pan and spread around the bottom. Bake for 5 minutes. Remove from oven. Pour the apple mixture over the baked batter. Spoon the rest of the batter over the apples and spread evenly, making sure the batter touches the edges of the pan. Bake 20-25 minutes. Cut in wedges. Serve warm.

FAMILY WHOLE WHEAT PANCAKES

¾ cup whole wheat flour
2 teaspoons baking powder
½ teaspoon salt
1 tablespoon honey
1 cup milk (whole milk or buttermilk)
1 tablespoon oil
1 egg, beaten or 1 tablespoon mashed tofu

Mix the dry ingredients together in one bowl and the liquid ingredients in another. Add milk mixture to flour mixture, and stir just until moistened (any lumps will disappear during cooking). Pour by spoonfuls into heated, oiled skillet. Flip over when bubbles come to the top. These are ready when a golden color appears. Top with fruit or preserves.

BERRY GOOD OATMEAL

1 cup old-fashioned oats
2 cups water
¼ cup blueberries
½ cup apple juice

Bring water to boil. Sprinkle oats into water while stirring constantly. Cover and simmer 15-20 minutes. Remove from heat. Add berries and apple juice. Serves 2.

SPECIAL DAY CEREAL

1 scoop frozen yogurt
¾ cup granola or Familia
½ cup fruit (peaches, berries, bananas, strawberries)
¼ cup milk or yogurt

Put yogurt in cereal bowl. Cover with granola or Familia, fruit and milk.

AVOCADO & CHEESE SANDWICH

Whole wheat toast
Safflower mayonnaise (optional)
Provolone cheese slices
Avocado slices
Tomato slices
Alfalfa sprouts or lettuce
Grated carrot

Spread the toast with mayonnaise and add the cheese, avocado, tomato, sprouts and grated carrot. Cut in half and serve.

To serve a toddler, make this an open-faced sandwich on one piece of toast and cut into fourths. Depending upon the age of the child, a lot of the sandwich will fall off. If this frustrates your child, you might try mashing up the avocado, bits of tomato, sprouts and grated carrot to make a sandwich spread to put on the toast. Don't forget to add the cheese and mayonnaise.

GREEK PITA SANDWICH

Cut open a piece of whole wheat pita bread so you have two flat pizza-like circles. Top each half with:

Green pepper
Onion
Tomato
Mung bean sprouts
Sliced mushrooms

Top with grated mozzarella cheese and pop into a broiler till cheese melts.

EGG SALAD SANDWICH

2 hard-boiled eggs, chopped
1 tablespoon celery, chopped
1 tablespoon onion, chopped
Safflower mayonnaise
Vegetable salt
Alfalfa sprouts
Provolone cheese, shredded

Combine egg, celery and onion in a small bowl with enough mayonnaise to bind together. Add vegetable salt to taste. Serve on pita bread, whole wheat toast or a bagel. This is good topped with sprouts and cheese.

CHICK PEA DELIGHT

2 cups cooked garbanzo beans
1 small clove garlic, crushed
2 tablespoons chopped onion (green onions add color)
2 tablespoons chopped green pepper or 2 tablespoons chopped celery or
*   both*
6 ounces tofu, drained
2 tablespoons soy sauce or 1 tablespoon tamari sauce
3 tablespoons safflower mayonnaise

Mash garbanzo beans with a fork or quickly blend in blender or food processor. Add remaining ingredients and mix thoroughly.

This spread is delicious on whole wheat toast with cheese, tomato and sprouts or lettuce. It is also good served in whole wheat pita bread.

WHOLE WHEAT BREAD

1 tablespoon dry yeast
2½ cups warm water
3 tablespoons honey
3 tablespoons safflower oil
2 teaspoons sea salt
6 cups whole wheat flour

Dissolve yeast in water with 1 tablespoon of the honey. When bubbles rise to surface (2-3 minutes) add remaining 2 tablespoons honey and the oil. Mix salt and flour and add to mixture, about 1 cup at a time (use a wooden spoon for stirring). Knead for 10 minutes. Cover and let rise till double in bulk. Punch down, separate into two greased loaf pans. Cover and let rise again (1 hour). Bake 30 minutes at 350°F.

SUNFLOWER BREAD

> 2 tablespoons oil
> 1 cup maple syrup or rice syrup
> 1 egg
> ¾ cup fresh orange juice
> 2 tablespoons grated orange rind
> 1 tablespoon baking powder
> ½ teaspoon salt
> 2 cups whole wheat flour
> 1 cup sunflower seeds, raw or toasted

Preheat oven to 325°F. Beat oil, maple syrup or rice syrup and egg with electric mixer for 1 minute in a medium bowl. Combine remaining ingredients in a small bowl. Add to first mixture all at once. Mix well with a wooden spoon just until smooth. Pour into greased loaf pan. Bake for 1 hour. Let cool in pan on rack 10 to 15 minutes. Turn out on rack to finish cooling. Wrap tightly to store.

SESAME SEED SALAD DRESSING

> ⅓ cup honey
> ½ teaspoon paprika
> ½ teaspoon salt
> ¼ teaspoon dry mustard
> 1 teaspoon onion juice or finely grated onion
> ½ teaspoon Worcestershire sauce
> 1 cup oil
> ½ cup cider vinegar
> 1 tablespoon toasted sesame seeds

Blend all ingredients except sesame seeds in blender. Add seeds and mix with a spoon. This is a great "sweet and sour" dressing—especially good on spinach salads and falafel.

TABOULIE

1½ cups bulgur wheat
¾ cup hot water
3 green onions, chopped
2 carrots, chopped
2 stalks celery, chopped
2 large tomatoes, chopped
⅓ cup safflower oil
¼ cup lemon juice
½ teaspoon sea salt
2 tablespoons chopped mint (optional)
2 tablespoons chopped parsley (optional)
½ cup fresh alfalfa sprouts

Place bulgur in a large bowl. Add hot water, cover and let stand while vegetables are being chopped. Prepare vegetables and add to the bulgur. Mix oil, lemon juice and salt together and pour over the bulgur mixture. Chill at least 1 hour. Top with sprouts at serving time.

SPINACH SALAD

Spinach pieces, washed and dried
Mushrooms, sliced
Green onions, chopped
Mung bean sprouts
Hard-boiled egg, sliced (optional)
Provolone cheese, grated

Toss all ingredients with Sesame Seed Salad Dressing and serve.

A toddler might like a plate with all these ingredients separated. Onions might not be a favorite with most, and the cheese could be cubed instead of grated.

ANTIPASTO SALAD

1 cup fresh cauliflower, in bite-size pieces
½ cup pitted black olives
1 small onion, sliced
½ cup cooked garbanzo beans
2 small tomatoes, quartered
½ cup grated carrot or 2 carrots cut into thin strips
2 hard-boiled eggs, quartered
4 slices provolone cheese, cut in strips
3 cups leaf or Bibb lettuce, torn in small pieces

Marinade
½ cup olive or safflower oil
¼ cup vinegar
½ teaspoon sea salt
Pinch oregano
1 garlic clove

Mix all marinade ingredients. Put cauliflower, olives, onion slices and garbanzo beans in a dish and cover with the marinade. Refrigerate 8 hours or overnight. Drain and reserve marinade. Arrange vegetables over lettuce pieces and add remaining ingredients. Toss lightly. Cover with remaining marinade or your favorite vinaigrette dressing.

POTATO SALAD

6 or 7 medium potatoes
1 medium onion, chopped
2 hard-boiled eggs, sliced
½ cup safflower mayonnaise
1 teaspoon sea salt
¼ cup sunflower seeds

Cook potatoes in their skins, then pare and dice into bite-size pieces. Add onion, eggs, mayonnaise and salt. Mix gently. Sprinkle sunflower seeds over the top and chill well before serving. This is a very refreshing summer salad.

SPROUTS SALAD

1 cup alfalfa sprouts
½ cup sunflower seeds, toasted
2 cups leaf and romaine lettuce
6 radishes, sliced or 1 cup radish sprouts
½ cucumber, sliced

Dressing
¼ cup oil
2 tablespoons cider, balsamic or red wine vinegar
⅛ teaspoon salt

Toss salad ingredients together. Make dressing with oil, vinegar and salt. Pour over salad and serve.

SUMMER SALAD DRESSING

1 tomato, quartered
1 cucumber, peeled and quartered
2 green onions (or 2 tablespoons chives)
½ cup oil
2 tablespoons red wine vinegar
⅛ teaspoon sea salt
1 clove garlic, chopped

Blend all ingredients in the blender and chill 1 hour. Pour over tossed salad and enjoy.

APPLE SALAD

Apples
Celery, chopped
Walnuts
Raisins
Mayonnaise or yogurt

Wash and chop apples into bite-size pieces. Add celery, walnuts and raisins. Add mayonnaise or yogurt and chill for 1 hour.

FRUIT SALAD
Grapes
Bananas
Oranges
Apples
Pineapple
Raisins
Coconut
Melon
Watermelon
Pears

Wash fruit and chop into bite-size pieces. Toss all fruit together in a large bowl and serve.

SPINACH DIP
1 large bunch spinach (about 1 lb.) steamed lightly
½ cup chopped green onions
1 tablespoon parsley (optional)
½ teaspoon dill weed
1 cup yogurt or sour cream
1 cup mayonnaise
1 tablespoon lemon juice
¼ teaspoon chives
Dash thyme
¼ teaspoon salt

Blend all ingredients in blender. Chill in refrigerator overnight. Serve with your favorite fresh vegetables.

VEGGIE PLATTER
Broccoli florets
Cauliflowerettes
Carrot sticks
Celery sticks
Green onions
Cherry tomatoes
Zucchini pieces
Mushroom slices
Radishes

Wash and prepare vegetables and arrange on a bed of lettuce. Serve with your favorite dip.

GUACAMOLE

>1 *ripe avocado*
>1 *tablespoon lemon juice*
>1 *small tomato, diced*
>1 *clove garlic, crushed*
>½ *teaspoon chili powder*
>*Dash Tabasco sauce*

Mash avocado with a fork. Add remaining ingredients and blend well. Chill 1 hour and serve with tortilla chips.

POTATO SOUP

>¼ *cup oil*
>1 *onion, chopped*
>3 *carrots, grated*
>1 *stalk celery, chopped*
>7-8 *potatoes, diced (wash well and leave skins on)*
>1 *quart stock or water*
>1 *teaspoon vegetable salt*
>1½ *cups noninstant dry milk powder*
>½ *cup milk*
>*Grated cheddar cheese or chives, chopped (optional)*

Saute onion, carrots, celery and potatoes in oil until tender. Pour in stock and add vegetable salt. Bring to boil; simmer 1 hour or cook 15 minutes in a pressure cooker. Add dry milk powder to 2 cups of soup liquid and the ½ cup milk and blend quickly in blender until milk powder is dissolved. Add to the soup and simmer 5 minutes. Serve topped with grated cheddar cheese or a sprinkling of chopped chives. Serves 4.

CUCUMBER SOUP

4 cups cucumber, chopped
2 cups water
2 cups yogurt or sour cream
1 clove garlic, minced
1 tablespoon honey
1 teaspoon sea salt
¼ teaspoon dill
1 green onion, chopped

Put all ingredients into blender or food processor and puree. Chill and serve. Serves 4.

LENTIL SOUP

2 tablespoons oil
2 cloves garlic, chopped
1 large onion, chopped
1 large carrot, grated
2 large potatoes, chopped small
1 cup washed lentils
3 cups tomato juice or 1 large (28 oz.) can tomatoes
3 cups water or stock
Thyme
Vegetable salt
Optionals: corn, peas, grated Swiss cheese

Saute garlic, onion, carrot and potatoes in oil. Add remaining ingredients (adding thyme and vegetable salt to taste). Bring to a boil, then simmer 1 hour. Top with grated Swiss cheese.

This is our favorite soup recipe. If you've never tried lentils before, this is the perfect recipe to quickly learn to like this little bean! Serve with a good bread or corn tortillas—it makes a hearty meal.

MISO SOUP

1 tablespoon olive oil
1 zucchini, sliced
1 carrot, grated
1 clove garlic, chopped
1 small onion, chopped
4 or 5 mushrooms, sliced
2 tablespoons miso (the garbanzo-flavored miso is our favorite)
4 cups water
1 teaspoon red wine vinegar
½ teaspoon honey
¼ teaspoon sesame oil
4 ounces tofu, cut in cubes
¼ cup scallions, chopped

Saute zucchini, carrot, garlic, onion, and mushrooms in oil. In a bowl, dissolve miso in water. Add to cooked vegetables.

Gently stir in vinegar, honey and sesame oil. Cover and simmer gently for 15 minutes. Add tofu and simmer one more minute. Sprinkle in the scallions and serve. Makes 2-3 servings.

FAMILY PIZZA

Crust:
1 tablespoon dry yeast
1¼ cups warm water
1 teaspoon honey
2 tablespoons oil
1½ teaspoons salt
3 to 3½ cups flour (whole wheat or combination of unbleached and whole wheat)

Sauce:
2 tablespoons olive oil
2 cloves garlic
1 large onion, chopped
½ green pepper, chopped
1 28-ounce can tomatoes
1 12-ounce can tomato puree
Oregano

Salt
Pepper
Garlic powder
Basil
½ teaspoon baking soda

Cheese:
Mozzarella, shredded
Provolone, shredded

Dissolve yeast in water with honey. When yeast makes bubbles on surface, add oil and salt. Add flour a bit at a time—enough to make a stiff dough. Knead 10 minutes and let rise 1½ hours.

Saute garlic, onion and pepper in oil. Add remaining ingredients except baking soda. Bring to a boil, then sprinkle on baking soda and stir in. Simmer 1-2 hours.

Punch dough down and spread out on two pizza pans. (Grease pan first.) Spread with sauce, add cheeses. Bake 15 minutes in preheated 425°F oven.

MOLLY'S TASTY TORTILLAS
(a great favorite with teenagers)

4 whole wheat tortillas
1½ cups cheese, grated
Lettuce
Tomato slices (optional)

Divide ingredients evenly over each tortilla. Broil for 5-10 minutes (until cheese melts). Take them out of the oven, roll them up and enjoy!

CALZONE

Dough:
1 tablespoon yeast
2 tablespoons honey
2 cups warm water
1 tablespoon salt
5½ to 6 cups flour

Filling:
1 lb. ricotta cheese
1 lb. lightly steamed spinach
2 cups grated mozzarella cheese
½ cup grated Parmesan cheese
1 tablespoon olive oil
2 cloves garlic, crushed
½ cup minced onion
Salt
Pepper
Dash of nutmeg

Dough: Dissolve yeast in water with honey. Add salt and flour. Knead 10 to 15 minutes. Cover and set to rise 1 hour while you prepare filling.
Filling: Saute garlic and onion in oil while steaming spinach in a steam basket or in a skillet with a tablespoon of water. Drain spinach and place in a large bowl. Gently mix in the three cheeses with the spinach. Add the sauteed garlic and onion.

When dough has risen, punch down and divide into 8 to 10 balls. Roll each ball out into a circle ¼ inch thick. Fill with ½ to ¾ cup filling. (Place filling on half of circle, fold over and make a ½-inch rim.) Moisten edges with water to help keep firmly closed. "Crimp" with a fork (by pressing down the tines all along the edges) and prick the top several times with the fork to let steam out during the baking. Bake on an oiled baking sheet at 450°F for 15 to 20 minutes. Brush with melted butter as soon as they come out of the oven. Makes 8 to 10 calzone.

This is a very special meal and is great served with a tossed salad.

SPAGHETTI SAUCE

2 tablespoons olive oil
2 cloves garlic, chopped
1 large onion, chopped
1 stalk celery, chopped
1 large carrot, grated
½ zucchini, grated
1 28-ounce can tomatoes
1 16-ounce can tomato sauce
1 6-ounce can tomato paste
½ cup water

Oregano
Basil
Salt
Pepper
Garlic salt

Saute the first five ingredients in oil until onions are translucent. Add remaining ingredients, seasoning to taste. Simmer 2-3 hours. Add mushrooms during the last half hour if you wish. (Don't let the carrots and zucchini scare you away from this recipe; they add a lot of vitamins and fullness to the sauce and it tastes almost the same as "regular" spaghetti sauce.)

SPAGHETTI SQUASH

1 large spaghetti squash
1 quart spaghetti sauce (page 121)

Wash squash and pat dry with a towel. Pierce the skin of the squash several times with the point of a knife or the tines of a fork. Place on a cookie sheet and bake at 350°F for 1¼ to 1½ hours. (Test for tenderness by piercing with a fork.) Remove squash from the oven and cut lengthwise. Gently scoop out "spaghetti" strands and place in a large bowl. Cover with your favorite spaghetti sauce and sprinkle with grated Parmesan cheese. This is a delightful "natural" dinner everyone will enjoy! This is also a great spaghetti substitute for those allergic to wheat or eggs.

LASAGNA

1 pound lasagna noodles
16 ounces ricotta cheese or tofu or a mixture of both
2 eggs
Dash cinnamon
Dash nutmeg
½ teaspoon parsley (optional)
2 cups shredded mozzarella cheese
1½ to 2 quarts spaghetti sauce
Grated Parmesan cheese

Cook lasagna noodles while preparing cheeses. In a large bowl, combine ricotta cheese, eggs, cinnamon, nutmeg and parsley and mix well. Set aside. Shred mozzarella cheese and place in another bowl. Have spaghetti sauce ready. Preheat oven to 350°F. In a large flat baking dish (oblong cake pans work well) place a layer of sauce, a layer of noodles, the ricotta cheese mixture (spread evenly over noodles), a layer of sauce, another layer of noodles, a layer of mozzarella cheese, a layer of sauce, another layer of noodles, more sauce, then sprinkle the top with Parmesan cheese. Bake at 350°F for 45 minutes. Cool 15 minutes before cutting.

Spinach Lasagna: Follow above recipe but add a layer of steamed spinach (about a half pound) and ¼ cup sauteed chopped onions. Sprinkle ¼ cup Parmesan cheese over the spinach layer before adding the sauce.

EGGPLANT PARMESAN

1 medium eggplant
⅓ cup unbleached or whole wheat flour
½ teaspoon sea salt
⅛ teaspoon cayenne pepper
1 tablespoon grated Parmesan cheese
2 tablespoons whole wheat bread crumbs
¼ teaspoon dried parsley
1 egg
2 tablespoons milk
2 tablespoons oil
2 cups spaghetti sauce (see page 121)
1 cup shredded mozzarella cheese
¼ cup finely grated Parmesan cheese

Slice eggplant into ½-inch slices. Combine flour, salt, pepper, cheese, bread crumbs and parsley. Mix egg and milk in a small bowl. Dip each eggplant slice into egg mixture, then the flour mixture, and then place in oiled skillet. Saute eggplant until lightly browned on each side, then drain slices on a paper towel. Arrange eggplant slices on a baking dish over one-half the spaghetti sauce. Pour remaining sauce over the top, then sprinkle with cheeses. Bake at 350°F for 20-30 minutes. Serves 4.

SPINACH SEASHELLS

¼ cup chopped onion
1 clove garlic, crushed
1 tablespoon oil
1 lb. fresh, washed spinach, chopped
1 lb. ricotta cheese
10 ounces mozzarella cheese, shredded
⅓ cup grated Parmesan cheese
2 eggs, beaten
1 teaspoon sea salt
½ teaspoon oregano
1 quart spaghetti sauce
8 ounces large seashell pasta

Saute onion and garlic in oil until soft. Add spinach and steam lightly. In large bowl, combine cheeses, eggs, salt and oregano. Gently stir in drained spinach mixture. Fill shells with spinach-cheese mixture and arrange in oiled baking dish (9" × 13"). Cover with spaghetti sauce. Bake at 350°F for 40 minutes. Serves 4.

ENCHILADA BAKE

1 small onion, chopped
1 clove garlic, crushed
½ green pepper, chopped
½ cup mushrooms, sliced (optional)
3 tablespoons oil
1 28-ounce can whole tomatoes
1 teaspoon ground cumin (optional)
2 teaspoons chili powder
½ teaspoon salt
6 corn tortillas
1½ to 2 cups cooked black (turtle) beans
1 cup shredded Monterey jack cheese
1 cup ricotta cheese or ½ cup ricotta and ½ cup tofu
Black olives, sliced (optional)

Saute onion, garlic, green pepper and mushrooms in the oil. Add tomatoes, cumin, chili powder and salt, and simmer for 30 minutes. Line an oiled casserole dish with three corn tortillas, half of the beans, half of the sauce, half of the ricotta, and half of the Monterey Jack cheese. Repeat layers. Sprinkle sliced olives over the top. Bake at 350°F, uncovered, for 20 minutes.

MEXICAN POTATO BAKE

4 baked potatoes
2 cups refried black beans
1 cup shredded Cheddar cheese

Cut baked potatoes lengthwise. Place ½ cup of the beans in each potato, then top with ¼ cup cheese. Return to the oven for 5 minutes until the cheese melts.

BROCCOLI QUICHE

Pastry for 9-inch pie
1 cup grated Swiss cheese
1 tablespoon finely chopped onion
1 cup steamed broccoli
¼ cup sauteed mushrooms (optional)
4 eggs
1¾ cups cream or milk
½ teaspoon salt
⅛ teaspoon cayenne pepper
¼ teaspoon honey

Prepare pastry and line a 9-inch pie pan or quiche dish. Sprinkle cheese, onion, broccoli and mushrooms into pie pan. Beat eggs with a fork, add remaining ingredients to eggs and mix. Pour into pie pan. Bake 15 minutes at 425°F, then 30 minutes at 300°F. Quiche is done when a knife inserted 1 inch from the edge comes out clean. Let quiche stand 10 minutes before cutting. This is excellent served with a salad and muffins.

CRUSTLESS QUICHE

½ cup sliced mushrooms
½ cup chopped onion
1 zucchini, chopped
1 clove garlic, chopped
2 tablespoons oil
5 eggs
⅓ cup milk
½ teaspoon sea salt
4 ounces cream cheese, cut into small cubes
1 cup grated Cheddar cheese
1 cup whole wheat bread cubes

Saute mushrooms, onion, zucchini and garlic in oil for 5 minutes. Combines eggs, milk and salt in a small bowl and mix lightly. Gently stir in cheese, then add bread cubes. Pour into oiled 9-inch pie pan. Bake at 350°F for 45 minutes. Let stand 5 minutes before serving. Serves 4.

FALAFEL BURGERS

¼ cup chopped onion
1 clove garlic, crushed
2 tablespoons oil
2 cups cooked garbanzo beans
2 potatoes, cooked
2 tablespoons sesame butter
1 tablespoon lemon juice
1 tablespoon noninstant dry milk
2 teaspoons soy sauce
1 tablespoon chopped parsley (optional)
½ teaspoon chili powder (optional)

Saute onion and garlic in oil. Mash garbanzo beans and potatoes with a fork or puree in blender or food processor. Add sauteed onion and garlic, sesame butter, lemon juice, dry milk, soy sauce, parsley and chili powder.

Shape into patties and place on oiled cookie sheet. Bake in 350°F oven 10 minutes on each side. Serve in pita bread with lettuce, tomato and cucumber. Sesame seed dressing can be drizzled over sandwich for added flavor.

Note: Falafel is a Middle Eastern food usually served on pita bread. This recipe can also be made into garbanzo balls and served as an appetizer or hors d'oeuvre.

CABBAGE, ZUCCHINI & TOMATO BAKE

½ cup chopped onion
1 tablespoon oil
1 head cabbage, chopped
2 zucchini, chopped
1 28-ounce can tomatoes

Saute onion in oil until soft. Add cabbage and zucchini and steam for 10 minutes. (Add a bit of water to help steaming process if necessary.) Add tomatoes. Turn into lightly oiled casserole dish and bake 45 minutes in 350°F oven.

EASY SCALLOPED POTATOES

5 potatoes, sliced thin
2 tablespoons chopped onion
2½ cups milk
2 tablespoons flour (optional)
1 tablespoon butter
1 teaspoon sea salt

Place half of the potatoes in an oiled baking dish. Sprinkle with half of the onion, flour, salt, butter and milk. Add remaining potatoes and the rest of the ingredients. Cover and bake at 350°F for 1 hour. Uncover and bake 30 minutes longer.

ZUCCHINI CHEESE BAKE

2 medium zucchini, sliced
2 large tomatoes, chopped
1 16-ounce can tomato sauce
½ teaspoon thyme
½ cup shredded provolone
1 clove garlic, minced

Combine all ingredients in an oiled baking dish. Bake at 350°F for 45 minutes. Serves 4.

BROILED ZUCCHINI

1 zucchini
¼ cup shredded Monterey Jack cheese
1 tablespoon grated Parmesan cheese

Wash and slice zucchini in ¼-inch pieces. Lightly steam in a steam basket or skillet for 5 minutes. Place zucchini slices on a foil-lined pie pan. Sprinkle with Monterey Jack, then with Parmesan. Broil 5-7 minutes or until cheese melts. Serves 2.

STUFFED BAKED ZUCCHINI

2 medium zucchini
2 tablespoons oil
½ cup chopped onion
½ cup sunflower seeds, chopped
¾ cup yogurt
2 teaspoons lemon juice
¼ teaspoon sea salt
½ cup whole wheat bread crumbs or ½ cup cooked brown rice
½ teaspoon chopped parsley
1 tomato, chopped

Slice zucchini in half and scoop out the center, leaving a firm shell. Reserve the inside pulp. Saute onion in oil until soft. Add the zucchini pulp and cook for 5 minutes. Add remaining ingredients and cook 5 more minutes. Spoon mixture back into zucchini shells and bake at 350°F for 20-30 minutes.

CHEESY CREAMY SPINACH

2 tablespoons butter
2 tablespoons flour
1½ cups milk
Dash cayenne pepper
⅛ teaspoon nutmeg
½ cup Parmesan cheese
1 pound fresh spinach, chopped
1 small onion, chopped
1 tablespoon oil

Make a white sauce with the first six ingredients by melting butter in a saucepan, then adding flour to make a paste. Slowly add milk and mix with a wire whip or a wooden spoon. Add cayenne, nutmeg and cheese and simmer 2 minutes. Pour over steamed spinach.

To steam spinach: Wash spinach and drain well. Saute onion in oil for 3 minutes, then add spinach and steam for 3 more minutes.

ZACHARY'S PEANUT BUTTER BALLS

(taken from Zac's early kitchen adventures and in his own words . . .)

1 cup peanut butter
½ cup dry milk (not instant kind)
Some wheat germ (Mom says about ½ cup)
Some sesame seeds (about ⅓ cup)
¼ cup honey
Dash of vanilla

"Mix everything up all together real good. Roll them up into little balls. Put them in the refrigerator. Yummy! You can put raisins in them; my sister likes them like that, but I don't."

Variations:
1. Add ¼ cup carob chips and call the recipe "Peanut Butter Candy."
2. Instead of shaping into balls, press mixture into a square baking dish. Chill. Cut into "Peanut Butter Bars."

CAITLIN'S BERRIES 'N CREAM

1 cup berries (strawberries, blackberries, blueberries, raspberries)
½ cup heavy cream
1 tablespoon honey
⅛ teaspoon vanilla extract

Wash berries and place them in a small bowl. Mix cream, honey and vanilla together and pour over berries. Enjoy!

RED, WHITE AND BLUE SPECIAL

Frozen yogurt
Blueberries
Strawberries
Whipped cream

Cover yogurt with fruit and top with whipped cream. Great for the Fourth of July.

TROPICAL BANANA SUNDAE

1 banana, sliced
1 tablespoon shredded fresh coconut
¼ cup milk or yogurt
1 tablespoon honey
Dash cinnamon

Mix all ingredients together in a small bowl. Serves 1.

ORANGE FRUIT PUNCH

1 quart orange juice
½ apple, cored and pared
1 tablespoon lemon juice
¼ cup strawberries
1 tablespoon honey

Blend all ingredients in a blender and serve over ice. Serves 4.

ZACHARY'S OWN SHAKE

1 ½ *cups milk*
1 *tablespoon carob powder*
1 *tablespoon honey*
1 *banana*
¼ *teaspoon lecithin*
¼ *teaspoon vanilla extract*
2 *tablespoons peanut butter*

Mix all ingredients in blender on high speed until smooth and creamy. (This recipe was truly invented by Zac when he was eight years old.)

FRUIT PUNCHES

Try these delicious juice combinations for a refreshing beverage:

orange/banana/papaya
orange/lemonade/pineapple
orange/lemonade/grape
orange/apricot/pineapple
grapefruit/cranberry
grapefruit/pineapple
lemonade/limeade
lemonade/orange/grape
cranberry/apple/pineapple
melon/banana/coconut
papaya/pineapple/orange
apricot/banana

Invent your own combinations!

For special occasions or as a substitute for alcoholic beverages (good for pregnant women), try mixing your favorite juice(s) with a sparkling naturally carbonated water.

TAMARI NUT MIX

2 *cups sunflower seeds*
1 *cup pumpkin seeds*
½ *cup tamari sauce*

Mix seeds with tamari sauce and let stand for 30 minutes. Bake on a baking sheet at 300°F for 15 minutes, stirring twice. Cool and store in airtight container. Delicious served with your favorite sandwich or just as a snack.

FRUIT LEATHER

1 pound very ripe fruit (apples, apricots, peaches, pears, strawberries)
1 tablespoon honey

Wash, peel and core fruit. Place fruit in blender or food processor and blend. Pour into saucepan, add honey and heat mixture just until it boils, stirring frequently. Cook for 3 minutes. Line cookie sheets with a layer of plastic wrap. Pour fruit onto plastic and spread into a thin layer. Carefully stretch a layer of cheesecloth over tray, being careful to keep it off the fruit mixture. Place tray in the hot sun for about 8 hours (or place in electric oven on lowest heat). Fruit leather is done when it can be peeled away from plastic wrap. This is a wonderful, natural, preservative-free treat everyone will love!

Chapter Thirteen

RECIPES FOR THE ALLERGIC CHILD

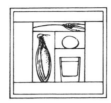

The following recipes offer ideas for the parent coping with nutritional needs of the allergic child. These recipes are free of one or all of the following common food allergens: eggs, milk and wheat. Be sure to check ingredients in recipes in all other sections of this book to find further foods for the allergic child.

NUT MILK

Use a blender to liquefy 2 ounces (⅓ to ½ cup) of sesame seeds, raw cashews or blanched almonds with 6 ounces (¾ cup) of water. This is good for making "milk" shakes.

SOY MILK

Blend ¼ cup tofu with ⅔ cup water in blender. Soy milk can be used for beverages or in baking.

SQUASH MILK

Dice and remove the seeds from a medium-sized yellow squash (but don't peel it). Measure 1¼ cups of the squash into blender jar. Pour in water just to cover the squash. Whirl in blender on high speed until smooth, 1-2 minutes. Strain. Makes about 1 cup. Good for baking, especially in spice cake or pumpkin pie.

NUT BUTTERS
(A peanut butter substitute for people who are allergic to peanuts)

> *1 cup ground nuts or seeds (almonds, sunflower seeds or sesame seeds)*
> *1 tablespoon safflower oil*

Lightly toast ground nuts or seeds in a 300°F oven, stirring often. Place ¼ cup ground nut meal in the blender with a small amount of oil. Blend at high speed for 5 seconds. Gradually add remaining nut meal (¼ cup at a time) and oil and continue to blend. Stir mixture before each addition of nuts (be sure blender is turned off). Store nut butter in a glass jar in refrigerator. Use as peanut butter substitute or as a delightful addition to the diet.

BANANA SHAKE

FREE OF: ● Egg   ● Milk   ● Wheat

> *1½ cups goat's milk* or nut milk*
> *1 banana*
> *Dash vanilla*

Blend in blender at high speed until smooth.

*Check with your doctor. Some children can tolerate goat's milk even though they are lactose intolerant.

TOFU MAYONNAISE

FREE OF: ● Egg   Milk   Wheat

> *8 ounces tofu*
> *2 tablespoons cider vinegar*
> *½ cup yogurt*
> *1 tablespoon fresh lemon juice*
> *1 teaspoon tamari**
> *1 tablespoon oil (safflower or olive)*
> *½ teaspoon dry mustard*
> *1 clove garlic, minced (optional)*

Puree all ingredients in blender or food processor until smooth. Store in jar with tight-fitting lid. Keeps in refrigerator for 1 week. Makes 1⅓ cups mayonnaise.

*For children on a wheat-free diet, omit tamari.

TOFU DIP

FREE OF: ● Egg   ● Milk   ● Wheat

> *8 ounces tofu*
> *4 teaspoons fresh lemon juice*
> *1 teaspoon onion juice or 1 clove garlic, minced*
> *¼ teaspoon dry mustard*
> *¼ teaspoon sea salt*
> *⅛ teaspoon celery seeds*

Drain tofu well. Blend all ingredients in blender. Chill 1 hour. Good as a dip for vegetables and crackers and as a sour cream substitute on baked potatoes.

PEANUT BUTTER-TOFU DELUXE

FREE OF: ● Egg   ● Milk   ● Wheat

> *8 ounces tofu, drained*
> *½ cup peanut butter*
> *1 tablespoon honey*
> *1 banana, mashed*
> *¼ cup sunflower seeds, chopped (optional)*
> *¼ cup raisins (optional)*

Blend tofu, peanut butter, honey and banana in blender or food processor. Add sunflower seeds and raisins if desired. Great on rice cakes or wheat-free crackers.

JOSH'S TOFU PANCAKES

FREE OF:	● Egg	● Milk	Wheat

¼ cup crumbled tofu
1½ cups water
1 tablespoon maple syrup
1 teaspoon vanilla extract
¼ cup oil
1½ cups whole wheat flour
1½ teaspoons baking powder

Blend tofu and liquid ingredients in blender until smooth. Mix flour and baking powder in medium bowl. Stir in liquid ingredients, mixing in gently just until the dry ingredients are moistened. Grease and heat a griddle or skillet. Drop batter from a large spoon onto griddle, lightly spreading each cake with the back of a spoon to make a round cake. Cook until bottom of pancake is golden brown and edges of pancake begin to look dry. With spatula or pancake turner, loosen and turn cake, brown other side. Serve at once with maple syrup or apple butter.

BUCKWHEAT PANCAKES

FREE OF:	Egg	● Milk	Wheat

1½ cups buckwheat flour
2½ teaspoons baking powder
½ teaspoon sea salt
¼ cup safflower oil
¾ cup water
2 eggs, beaten
2 tablespoons honey

Combine all dry ingredients in a large bowl. Mix oil, water, eggs and honey. Stir liquid ingredients into the dry ingredients. Pour batter onto oiled griddle or skillet. Flip when brown on one side. Serves 3-4.

RICE PANCAKES

FREE OF: ● Egg   ● Milk   ● Wheat

2 cups cooked brown rice
2 cups tofu, drained and chopped
2 tablespoons lemon juice
1 teaspoon sea salt
2 tablespoons potato flour
¼ cup chopped walnuts (optional)

Mix rice and tofu together in a large bowl. Add remaining ingredients. Shape into 4-6 "pancakes" and cook in oiled skillet. Fry until golden on both sides. Delicious for breakfast, lunch or supper.

RICE WAFFLES

FREE OF: Egg   ● Milk   ● Wheat

2 cups rice flour
2 cups goat's milk* or diluted nondairy creamer (free of casein, sodium caseinate or lactalbumin)
4 teaspoons corn-free baking powder
½ teaspoon sea salt
¼ cup oil or milk-free margarine
2 eggs, separated

Mix all dry ingredients in a large bowl. Gently mix egg yolks with a fork then add the milk and oil to the egg yolks. Stir into dry ingredients. Beat egg whites until stiff and gently fold into batter. Cook on lightly oiled skillet or griddle. Serves 4.

*Check with your doctor. Some children can tolerate goat's milk even though they are lactose intolerant.

RYE BREAD

FREE OF: ● Egg   ● Milk   ● Wheat

1 tablespoon dry yeast
1¼ cups warm water
1 teaspoon honey
2 tablespoons safflower oil
4 cups rye flour
2 teaspoons salt
3 tablespoons caraway seeds (optional)

Dissolve yeast with water and honey. Add oil. Stir in dry ingredients, adding more water if necessary. Knead 10 minutes. Cover and let rise in a warm place for 1½ hours. Punch down. Knead 5 minutes, shape into 1 loaf and place in greased bread pan. Cover and let rise 30 minutes. Bake 1 hour and 10 minutes at 375°F.

WONDERFUL WHEAT BERRY BREAD

FREE OF: ● Egg   ● Milk   Wheat

¾ cup whole wheat berries
2 cups water
1 cup whole wheat flour
1 cup chopped nuts
1 teaspoon baking soda
1 teaspoon sea salt
½ cup crumbled tofu
½ cup water
¼ cup barley malt or maple syrup
2 tablespoons oil

Combine whole wheat berries and water in medium saucepan. Bring to boil over medium heat and boil for 2 minutes. Turn off heat, cover saucepan and let stand for 1-2 hours. Bring to boil again and simmer, uncovered, 1½ hours or until tender.

Preheat oven to 350°F. Mix flour, nuts, baking soda and salt in a large bowl. Place tofu, water, barley malt or maple syrup and oil in blender and blend until smooth. Stir tofu mixture into flour mixture and mix just until dry ingredients are moistened. Drain whole wheat berries and fold into bread mixture. Pour into greased bread pan. Bake 1 hour. Let cool in pan for 10 minutes, then turn out on wire rack to finish cooling.

BANANA NUT BREAD

FREE OF: Egg   ● Milk   ● Wheat

1½ cups banana, mashed
2 tablespoons water
2 eggs
1½ cups arrowroot flour
1 teaspoon soda
½ teaspoon sea salt
¾ cup chopped walnuts

Combine banana and water in a large bowl. Beat eggs, then mix with banana. Stir in dry ingredients and mix well. Add chopped nuts. Bake at 350°F for 45 minutes in a lightly greased bread pan.

OATMEAL BRAN MUFFINS

FREE OF: Egg   ● Milk   ● Wheat

1 cup oatmeal
1 cup bran or whole wheat flour
1 tablespoon baking powder
1 teaspoon baking soda
½ teaspoon sea salt
1 egg
3 tablespoons oil
2 tablespoons barley malt or molasses
1 cup soft tofu or soy yogurt
½ cup chopped nuts (toasted)
½ cup currants or raisins

Preheat oven to 425°F. Put the oatmeal, bran or flour, baking powder, baking soda and salt in a blender. Blend on high speed about 1 minute or until it looks like flour. Pour into a large mixing bowl. Put remaining ingredients, except nuts and currants, in blender and blend about 1 minute or until smooth. Pour blended mixture over oatmeal mixture; mix gently until all the dry ingredients are moistened. Stir in nuts and currants or raisins. Pour into greased or paper-lined muffin cups. (Cups will be about ¾ full.) Bake 15 minutes. Turn out onto wire rack to cool.

PEANUT BUTTER CAROB FUDGE

FREE OF: ● Egg   Milk   ● Wheat

> 1 cup peanut butter
> 1 cup honey
> ¾ cup toasted carob powder
> ¾ cup noninstant dry milk powder

Mix all ingredients together with a fork, then knead about 3 minutes to thoroughly combine mixture. Press into a 9″ × 9″ square pan and refrigerate several hours or overnight. Cut into squares and serve. Raisins can be added for a variation.

BANANA-OAT CAKE

FREE OF: Egg   ● Milk   ● Wheat

> 2 cups oat flour (or ground old-fashioned oats)
> 2 teaspoons corn-free baking powder
> ½ teaspoon sea salt
> 2 tablespoons safflower oil
> 2 eggs
> ⅓ cup honey
> 2 tablespoons water
> 2-3 bananas, mashed

Sift oat flour before measuring, then sift with baking powder and salt. Beat oil, eggs, honey and water in a small bowl. Add mashed banana to egg mixture and mix well. Combine liquid and dry ingredients together. Pour into greased 8″ × 8″ square pan and bake at 350°F for 30 minutes.

OATMEAL SHEET CAKE

FREE OF: ● Egg   ● Milk   ● Wheat

1 cup oat flour (or old-fashioned oats, ground fine)
1 tablespoon arrowroot
1 teaspoon cinnamon
1 teaspoon salt
½ teaspoon nutmeg
⅔ cup water
2 teaspoons corn-free baking powder
2 tablespoons safflower oil
1 banana, mashed
⅓ cup almonds or walnuts, chopped
¼ cup raisins

Mix all ingredients in a large bowl. Pour into greased 9″ × 9″ square baking pan. Bake at 350°F for 15-20 minutes.

Chapter Fourteen

WHAT NOT TO PUT INTO THE MOUTHS OF BABES

Over five million children are poisoned each year in the United States. Infants, toddlers and children need not be out of sight long before they can inhale or ingest a toxic substance. Consider these facts about poisoning:

- Poisonings are most likely to occur in children under five years of age, with one-year-olds accounting for the highest number of poisonings reported.
- There is an extremely high incidence of repeat poisonings. A child who is poisoned once probably will be poisoned again.
- A large number of ingested poisons are medications found within a child's reach or climb. (Give a toddler a chair, desk, toilet or table to stand or climb on and he probably will.)
- Many first-aid antidote charts and labels are incorrect or out of date. Often a well-meaning parent does more harm than good by following directions from an old chart rather than phoning the Poison Control Center or a physician first. In fact, the old remedy of giving salt water to induce vomiting has even caused death.
- *Never* give syrup of ipecac to induce vomiting unless directed to do so by the Poison Control Center or your health-care provider. Every medicine cabinet should contain a bottle of ipecac syrup. Check the expiration date to be sure your bottle is not outdated.
- You may have poison-proofed your home but the homes of friends and relatives may have poisons within reach. Be especially cautious of this fact.

FIRST AID FOR POISONING

Swallowed Poisons

If the person is awake and able to swallow, give water.
Call the poison center or your doctor.
Caution: Antidote charts and labels may be outdated and incorrect.
Do not give salt, vinegar, mustard, raw eggs or citrus juices.

Inhaled Poisons

Immediately drag or carry the person to fresh air.
Ventilate the area.
Call the poison center or your doctor.

Poisons on the Skin

Remove contaminated clothing and flood skin with water for fifteen minutes.
Wash gently with soap and water twice.
Call the poison center or your doctor.

Poisons in the Eye

Flush the eye with lukewarm (not hot) low-pressure water for fifteen to twenty minutes. Water can be poured from a pitcher held two to three inches from the eye. You need not force the eyelid open, but have the person blink while flushing.
Call the Poison Control Center or your health-care provider.
Have this information ready when you call the Poison Control Center:

- Your name and phone number
- Age and approximate weight of child
- Name of product and ingredients
- Amount ingested
- The container
- Symptoms
- Time poisoning occurred
- Any first aid already given

POISON-PROOFING YOUR HOME

1. Do you have the phone number of your Poison Control Center and/or physician by your phone(s)? If not, please put this book down

> Don't ever hesitate to call the Poison Control Center if you think your child may have ingested or inhaled a possible poison. Early treatment can save a life.

and do it now and circle these numbers for your babysitter. Your child is so precious!

2. Store all medicines and household cleaning supplies out of reach (and sight) of infants and children. Use locked cabinets or child-resistant safety latches when necessary. Try to buy the least toxic cleaners and keep all products in their original containers.

3. Request child-resistant caps on all medicines. Request extra child-resistant containers and transfer vitamins into them.

4. Never store medicine or any poisonous product in beverage or food containers. More than one unsuspecting child has picked up a soda bottle in the garage that was filled with gasoline or kerosene.

5. Never tell children that medicine tastes like candy or that foods you don't want them to eat or drink are "poison." Those unclear messages can cause confusion. For example, if too much medicine is taken because it tastes like candy, possible poisoning could be the result. It also is wise to take your own medicine when children aren't watching since they love to imitate grownups.

6. Check the dates of all drugs in your medicine cabinet and flush old pills down the toilet. Do not let your child play with empty medicine bottles.

7. Keep a bottle of ipecac syrup in your medicine cabinet. **Caution:** Use ipecac only if instructed to do so by the Poison Control Center or a physician. Follow their specific instructions for use.

8. Remember to keep all potential poisons out of reach when your child is away from home.

9. Be aware of which plants are poisonous. The following common plants and parts of plants are poisonous:

azalea	buckeye
acorns	buttercup
autumn crocus	caladium
baneberry	*castor bean
bittersweet	chokecherry
bleeding heart	crocus
boxwood	daffodil

dieffenbachia
elderberry
elephant ear
English ivy
four-o'clocks
*foxglove
golden chain
holly
hyacinth
iris
jequirity bean
jessamine
Jerusalem cherry
jimson weed
juniper
larkspur
laurel
lily of the valley
mistletoe
monkshood
morning glory
mushrooms
narcissus

nightshade
oak
oleander
periwinkle
philodendron
poison ivy
poison oak
poison sumac
pokeweed
poppy
privet
rhododendron
rhubarb leaves
rosary pea
shamrock
sweet pea
tobacco
tomato leaves
tulip
*water hemlock
*wild mushroom
wisteria
yew

Check with your Poison Control Center if you have a question about plants not listed above.

Beware . . . The following products can cause *poisoning*:

aftershave lotion
alcohol
ammonia
antifreeze
aspirin
automatic dishwashing
    compound
automotive products
bleach
charcoal lighter

chemicals
cigarettes
cleaning and disinfecting
    agents
cosmetics
cough medicine
drain cleaner
drugs (prescription or over-the-
    counter drugs, ointments or
    creams)

*especially toxic plants

furniture polish
gasoline
glues and adhesives
hair dyes and bleaches
insecticides
jewelry containing beans or
    seeds
kerosene
lye
mothballs
mouthwash
nail polishes and removers
oven cleaners

paint and paint thinners
perfumes
pesticides
petroleum products
plants
plastics
rat poison
rubbing alcohol
shampoo and soap
toilet bowl cleaner
vitamins and minerals
weed killer

Other products also can be harmful. When in doubt, consult the Poison Control Center in your area.

Curiosity killed the cat. Don't let it kill your child. Put all poisons out of the reach of children.

Bibliography

Baker, Catherine. *The Perfection Trap: College Age Women and Eating Disorders.* (Booklet) Durham, NC, 1992.

Ballentine, Rudolph, M.D. *Diet and Nutrition: A Holistic Approach.* Honesdale, PA: Himalayan International Institute, 1978.

Brody, Jane E. *Jane Brody's Nutrition Book.* New York: Bantam Books, 1982.

Castle, Sue. *The Complete New Guide to Preparing Baby Foods.* New York: Bantam, 1992.

Davis, Adelle. *Let's Cook It Right.* New York: NAL Dutton, 1988.

—*Let's Get Well.* New York: NAL Dutton, 1972.

—*Let's Have Healthy Children.* New York: NAL Dutton, 1981.

Dufty, William. *Sugar Blues.* New York: Warner Books, 1993.

Elmer-Dewitt, Philip. "Mad About Vitamins." *Time*, 1 November 1993, pp. 73-94.

Emerling, Carol G., and Eugene O. Jonckers. *The Allergy Cookbook: Delicious Recipes for Everyday and Special Occasions.* Garden City, NY: Doubleday & Company, 1969.

Ewald, Ellen. *Recipes for a Small Planet.* New York: Ballantine, 1985.

Feingold, Ben F. *Why Your Child Is Hyperactive.* New York: Random House, 1985.

Firkaly, Susan. "Nutrition in Pregnancy." *Baby Talk*, May 1987, p. 24.

Ford, Marjorie W., Susan Hillyard, and Mary Faulk Kooch. *The Deaf Smith Country Cookbook.* New York: Avery Publishers, 1991.

Goldbeck, Nikki, and David Goldbeck. *The Supermarket Handbook: Access to Whole Foods.* New York: NAL Dutton, 1976.

Golos, Natalie, and Frances Golos Golbita. *Coping with Your Allergies.* New York: Simon and Schuster, 1986.

Gordon, Richard A. *Anorexia and Bulimia: Anatomy of a Social Epidemic.*

Cambridge: Basil Blackwell, 1990.

Gorman, Christine. "Parents: Can the Juice!" *Time*, 11 April 1994, p. 64.

—"When Breast-Feeding Fails." *Time*, 22 August 1994, p. 63.

Harris, Mark. "Raising Healthy Veg Kids." *Vegetarian Times*, July 1994, pp. 58-65.

Hausman, Patricia, and Judith Benn Hurley. *The Healing Foods*. Emmaus, PA: Rodale Press, 1989.

Hirschfeld, Herman, M.D. *Understanding Your Allergy*. New York: Arco Publishing, 1979.*

Houben, Milton, and William Kropf, M.D. *Harmful Food Additives: The Eat-Safe Guide*. Port Washington, NY: Ashley Books, 1980.

La Leche League International Staff. *The Womanly Art of Breastfeeding: Thirty-Fifth Anniversary Edition*. New York: NAL Dutton, 1991.

Lappe, Frances Moore. *Diet for a Small Planet: Twentieth Anniversary Edition*. New York: Ballantine, 1991.

Margen, Sheldon, M.D., and the Editors of the University of California at Berkeley *Wellness Letter*. *The Wellness Encyclopedia of Food and Nutrition*. New York: Rebus, 1992.

Mindell, Earl. *Earl Mindell's Food as Medicine*. New York: Simon and Schuster, 1994.

—*Vitamin Bible*. New York: Warner Books, 1992.

Nonken, Pamela P., and S. Roger Hirsch, M.D. *The Allergy Cookbook and Food-Buying Guide*. New York: Warner Books, 1982.*

National Research Council. *Diet, Nutrition and Cancer*. Washington, DC: National Academy Press, 1982.

Newmark, Gretchen. "Eat That! Not!" *The Energy Times*, March/April 1994, pp. 40-44.

Ornish, Dean. *Dr. Dean Ornish's Program for Reversing Heart Disease*. New York: Random House, 1990.

Physicians Committee for Responsible Medicine. *Vegetarian Starter Kit*. Washington, DC., 1993.

Pryor, Karen. *Nursing Your Baby*. New York: Pocket Books, 1991.

Rapaport, Howard G., M.D. and Shirley M. Linde. *The Complete Allergy Guide*. New York: Simon and Schuster, 1970.

Rapp, Doris J., M.D. *Allergies and the Hyperactive Child*. New York: Sovereign Books, 1979.*

— *Allergies and Your Family*. New York: Practical Allergy Research Foundation, 1990.

— *Is This Your Child?* New York: William Morrow and Company, 1991.

Robertson, Laurel, Carol Flinders, and Brian Ruppenthal. *The New Laurel's Kitchen: A Handbook for Vegetarian Cookery and Nutrition*. Berkeley, CA: Ten Speed Press, 1986.

Sanders, Tab, and Sheela Reddy. "Vegetarian Diets and Children." *American Journal of Clinical Nutrition*. 59 (May 1994): pp. 1179-1182.

Sass, Lorna J. *Recipes from an Ecological Kitchen*. New York: Morrow, 1992.

Smith, Lendon H., M.D. *Feed Your Kids Right*. New York: Dell, 1981.

— *Foods for Healthy Kids*. New York: Berkeley Books, 1987.

Smith, Melanie M., and Fima Lifshitz, M.D. "Excess Fruit Juice Consumption as a Contributing Factor in Nonorganic Failure to Thrive." *Pediatrics* 93 (March 1994): pp. 438-43.

Thomas, Anna. *The Vegetarian Epicure*. New York: Vintage Books, 1972.

Toth, Robin. *Naturally It's Good . . . I Cooked It Myself!* White Hall, VA: Betterway Publications, 1982.*

— and Jacqueline Hostage. *Does Your Lunch Pack Punch?* White Hall, VA: Betterway Publications, 1983.*

United States Department of Agriculture. *Human Nutrition Information Service: The Food Guide Pyramid*. Home and Garden Bulletin Number 252. August 1992.

Weed, Susun S. *The Wise Woman Herbal for the Childbearing Years*. Woodstock, NY: Ash Tree, 1985.

Weisenthal, Debra Blake. "Herbs for Pregnancy." *Vegetarian Times*, June

1994, pp. 86-87.

Wunderlich, Ray C. *Improving Your Diet.* St. Petersburg, FL: Johnny Reads, 1976.*

Yntema, Sharon K. *Vegetarian Baby: A Sensible Guide for Parents.* Ithaca, NY: McBooks Press, 1991.

Yoga Fellowship Society. *Make It Light.* Boardman, OH: Nature's Nook, 1980.*

*Out of print at this writing but often available at your public library.

Other Recommended Reading

Allergy Cookbook, Ruth R. Shattuck, NAL Dutton, 1986.

EveryWoman's Health: The Complete Guide to Body and Mind by 18 Women Doctors, Douglas S. Thomson, ed., Prentice-Hall Press, 1985.

Feeding the Hungry Heart: The Experience of Compulsive Eating, Geneen Roth, Penguin Books, 1983.

Jewish Vegetarian Cooking, Rose Friedman, Thorsons, 1993.

The Kopan Cookbook: Vegetarian Recipes from a Tibetan Monastery, Betty Jung, Chronicle Books, 1992.

Prescription for Nutritional Healing, James F. Balch and Phyllis Balch, Avery Publishers, 1990.

Recipes for a Small Planet, Ellen Buckman Ewald, Ballantine Books, 1993.

Simply Vegan, Debra Wasserman and Reed Mangels, The Vegetarian Resource Group, 1991.

Student Eating Disorders, Michael P. Levine, National Education Association of the United States, 1987.

Vegetarian Journal, P.O. Box 570, Oak Park, IL 60303.

The Vegetarian Journal's Guide to Natural Foods Restaurants, The Vegetarian Resource Group, P.O. Box 1463, Baltimore, MD 21203.

Index

Recipe Index

Get the Most Out of Life
With These Great Books